AMERICAN SOCIETY FOR INDUSTRIAL SECURITY
1625 PRINCE STREET
ALEXANDRIA, VA 22314
(703) 519-6200

HOTEL & MOTEL SECURITY MANAGEMENT

Walter J. Buzby II and David Paine

Security World Publishing Co., Inc.
Los Angeles, California 90034

First Edition 1976

Second Printing 1978

Security World Publishing Co., Inc.
2639 South La Cienega Boulevard
Los Angeles, California 90034

Printed in the United States of America

Library of Congress Cataloging in Publication Data

Buzby, Walter J   1927-
    Hotel & motel security management.

    Includes index.
    1.   Hotels, taverns, etc.--Security measures.
2.   Motels--Security measures.   I.   Paine, David,
joint author.   II.   Title.
TX911.3.S4B89   647'.94   76-12555
ISBN 0-913708-24-0

Contents

iii

Needed · **The Fire Prevention Survey** · Housekeeping · Fire
Regulations · Extinguishing Equipment · Electrical Systems ·
Employee Training · Instructions to Guests · Reporting Systems
· Warnings · **Fire Bill** · Reporting a Fire · Operator Action ·
Personnel Assignments · Night Inspections · Room Record · Fire
Department Assistance ·Drills Needed · **Arson** · Organized Crime
Involvement · Financial Trouble as Motive · Hotel Arson
Incidents · **Disaster Protection** · Detailed Planning · Civil Defense

Introduction

Hotels and motels, large and small, are extremely vulnerable to security hazards. The very nature of their operation, which involves the presence of a wide selection of humanity, most of whom are unknown to the proprietor, in itself poses a considerable threat to the security of property. Risks of fire are also serious. The incidence of hotel fires causing loss of life and serious damage to property has increased in recent years, culminating in the disastrous affair at Seoul, Korea, where 163 persons lost their lives in 1971.

It will therefore be apparent that those who are in charge of the day-to-day operation of a hotel should at least be aware of some of the security problems involved and what measures can be taken to lessen the severity of the threat.

The hotel manager must also be aware of a much larger volume of legal provisions than would apply to the owner of a private home. He has a direct responsibility for the safety and well-being of his guests, and part of this responsibility is compliance with such laws as are in effect respecting the operation of hotels.

The purpose of this book is, therefore, to assist the hotel or motel manager, and others responsible for security in these facilities, by a discussion of some of the threats and countermeasures relative to security, together with a basic description of the laws affecting the hotel business. The text should enable hotel managers and security officers to gain a basic knowledge of the more important aspects of these laws and to discover the sources from which a more detailed study of them can be made.

Not all hotels and motels, of course, are of the 100-rooms-

and-up variety with large, specialized staffs. Many units are "one-man" or "family" operations with the owner or manager and a very limited number of employees filling all positions. For the small operation to have an employee delegated to handle nothing but security is out of the question. Yet the smaller establishment is confronted with the same problems as the large operation, and in some instances it has far more serious problems because wrongdoers are aware that it does not have a complete security force. In our attempts to call attention to security problems and to offer possible solutions, we have attempted also to indicate how the small operation might handle the same problem with a limited staff.

Also included in the text is material relating to the security of cash, food and beverages which may assist not only those in the hotel industry, but also restaurant owners and persons in charge of other catering establishments, with their security problems.

This book should be interpreted generally rather than specifically. Not all of our suggestions can be applied to individual establishments exactly as worded. Each location is different and poses its own special security problems. The ideas described in this book, however, can be adapted to meet the needs of hotels, motels or catering establishments, whether large or small.

Finally, it is urged that all establishments profit from the lessons to be learned from the tragic affair at the Howard Johnson's Hotel in New Orleans in 1973, which is repeatedly referred to in the text. The case is a shocking demonstration of how a security lapse can lead to a tragic and costly disaster.

— *The Authors*
1976

Chapter 1

The Hotel and the Security Function

The hotel security officer may be compared in many respects to a member of a law enforcement agency. His rights, duties and obligations are determined by the law of the land as well as by departmental regulations. Certain laws, statutes or ordinances apply only to hotels and hotel operations, so it is necessary that we understand exactly what a hotel is as far as our legal system is concerned. The terms hotel, inn, apartment, apartment hotel, boarding house, lodging house, or spa may appear almost synonymous to the uninformed, and it might be assumed that they would all be treated the same in the eyes of the law. Nothing could be further from the truth. For that reason, it is well that a short history of hotels and laws concerning them be considered.

HISTORY OF HOTELS

Today's hotel, where a guest may receive room, board and entertainment, is a far cry from the first public houses in Roman times and earlier. These public houses, actually the first hotels, filled a serious need for the people of those times and were considered a necessity by all. Whenever men traveled away from their own homes overnight, they needed a place of shelter. The highways were not conducive to the carrying of heavy loads in wagons; in addition, highwaymen made travel through certain parts of the country very dangerous, especially at night. The safest way to travel was with a strong, fast horse and a minimum of

1

baggage. The need for some type of shelter at convenient locations where the traveler could find refreshment and protection from thieves and robbers was obvious. So it was that local taverns and other inns began to cater to the traveling public.

Early Public Houses

The earliest public house was usually the home of the proprietor. It contained a large common hall with perhaps two separate chambers, one for the master of the house and one for the mistress. The common hall was the gathering place for all. Heated by a central fireplace and lighted by torch or candle, this room served all functions. By day it would be set with tables and chairs where all meals were served and entertainment could be conducted. Following the evening meal, the tables would be removed and the beds spread upon the floor. Servants and guests alike slept in this hall.

In some of the larger homes where there might be additional individual chambers, certain persons might be assigned to these smaller rooms. Seldom was a traveler permitted to occupy such a room by himself, however. Even the king, when traveling, was expected to share his room with another. In today's medical terminology, the best a traveler could hope for in early France or England was a "semi-private" room.

Travelers making use of such accommodations expected a certain standard of treatment in sleeping facilities, the refreshments available for them and their horses, and their personal safety. Naturally, they expected to pay a reasonable price for such services, but it soon became apparent that some innkeepers were not above charging excessive fees while providing only the barest minimum of services and no protection whatever. It became necessary for the government, by order of the king, to pass certain laws setting forth the duties and rights accorded the innkeeper as well as the rights and duties of the guest. Thus, the first laws concerning lodging for travelers came into existence. These laws would later become the Common Law upon which most of the New World law was based.

In early England, public houses were normally called "inns" or "taverns." Normally, the name "inn" was reserved for the finer establishments catering to the nobility and clergy. The houses frequented by the common man were known as "taverns." In France, a similar distinction was made, with the finer establishments known as *hotelleries* and the less pretentious houses called *cabarets.* After the Norman invasion, the word "hostel" was used to refer to all such public houses. To "host" was to put up at an inn, and the "hostler" was the officer charged with entertainment of the guests. In England, this person was the "innkeeper." The term "hostler" was later used to refer only to the keeper of the stable or the groom charged with care of the livery.

The word "hotel" came into use in England about 1760 and, over a period of approximately 80 years, came to denote "an inn of a superior kind." The word was introduced into the United States about 1797. Prior to that time the term "inn" or "coffeehouse" had been in general use in America. One of the earliest American lexicographers defines hotel as "an inn of a high grade, a respectable tavern." In 1864, Webster defines hotel as "an inn; a public house, especially one of some style or pretensions."

Travelers Protected by Law

Those first laws passed by royal decree were for the protection of the transient guest, the weary traveler who required food and shelter at once, as opposed to the occupant of a boarding house who desired to be more or less a permanent guest. Unlike the transient, the boarder was seeking a home and had time to bargain with his host for accommodations and charges. While the innkeeper may cater to permanent guests and make his inn attractive for them, he is nonetheless an innkeeper as long as he professes also to supply the needs of travelers, as do most hotel keepers today.

This distinction between the transient and the permanent or semi-permanent guest is a concept still considered by the courts. Historically, the Majority Rule in the United States set forth requisites for a public house to be considered a hotel as follows:

"An inn is a house where all who conduct themselves properly, and who are able and ready to pay for their entertainment, are received, if there is accommodation for them, and who, without any stipulated engagement as to the duration of their stay, or as to the rate of compensation, are, while there, supplied at a reasonable charge with their lodging, and such services and attention as are necessarily incident to the use of the house as a temporary home."

HOTELS AND THE LAW TODAY

Legal Definition of Hotel

In many states and provinces today, the word "hotel" is defined by statute; naturally, where such definition exists, it is controlling. We might summarize the current situation as follows:

1. "Inn," "hotel," "motel" and "motor inn" are synonymous.
2. An inn must be a place for the reception, refreshment, and entertainment of travelers. It necessarily follows that no one who does not use the inn for its proper purpose can claim to be a guest of the keeper of such inn and thereby be given the peculiar privileges which the law allows such a guest. In addition, unless he is a guest, the innkeeper cannot exercise against him the right of lien or other remedies which he is allowed as an innkeeper.
3. No house is held to be an inn which does not provide sleeping accommodations.
4. No matter what name is given to the establishment, if the proprietor is willing to entertain all comers to the best of his ability, and if he provides the specified essentials, the house will be considered a hotel.
5. An inn must be a house for the reception and entertainment of *all* travelers, so that the innkeeper has no right to refuse to receive any such persons for whom he has accommodations. If he claims a right to pick and choose his guests and exercises such right, he is not an innkeeper and his house is not an inn.

Basic Legal Requirements

While there are a number of laws, such as the Criminal Code, which apply to all businesses and individuals, there are also many laws that apply only to hotels, motels, innkeepers and their guests. In the chapters that follow, we will attempt to indicate how the law regulates the behavior and the business activities of all concerned with hotels. These laws will range from federal statutes to state or provincial laws and to local or municipal ordinances, codes or regulations. Naturally, these laws will vary in wording and content from country to country and state to state as well as city to city; however, the intent is normally approximately the same, and it will be our purpose to show only the intent of the law.

One legal concept that is believed to be universal among English-speaking nations is that the innkeeper has the right to make certain regulations and rules concerning the conduct of his own business—provided, of course, that these regulations are not in violation of the law. For example, a hotel regulation requiring men to wear jackets in a public cocktail lounge after 5:00 p.m. would be considered within the right of the innkeeper. Therefore, in addition to public law, the security officer will be concerned with those rules and regulations established by the owners of the property.

Those primarily involved in the management of a hotel generally have many responsibilities, most of which are inter-related, and some of which may cause a degree of conflict of interest. The requirements to observe the various laws relating to hotel operations and to maintain the security of the premises, its equipment, and the lives and property of guests, may to some extent pose a conflict of interest with the main objective of running a profitable operation. The reason for this is that the law and security *per se* tend to be restrictive to the wishes and desires of most people.

It will not be our attempt to resolve this conflict; rather we desire to make available some information that might assist in securing the desired results with the least amount of disruption to the commercial objectives inherent in the hotel business.

Overall Responsibility for Law and Security

The ultimate responsibility for legal and security require-ments will lie with the owner of the property. From the outset, these responsibilities must be clearly understood and a general policy must be formulated and set forth. The security officer must work within the guidelines of this policy. He will be required to answer the owners or top management for the responsibility of compliance with security and legal requirements. This principle, namely that the security officer's role is to implement protective measures and to advise top management on technical security matters, is common to industry in general; but the decision whether to implement protective measures at all is one for the senior executive.

HAZARDS TO SECURITY

Let us examine some of the security requirements that are inherent in the hotel industry, bearing in mind that our responsibility extends not only to the physical plant (the building), but also to the lives and property of every person in the building. The definition of "security" points this out clearly: "those measures required to promote a state of well-being relative to an establishment, to protect life and property and to minimize the risks of natural or man-made disasters or crime." These hazards may include, among others: fire, flood, earthquake, hurricane, epidemic, civil disorder, bombing, sabotage, theft and fraud.

As we consider the hazards, we must determine what effect each may have on the various segments of our operation—the building itself and its surroundings, the supplies and equipment within the building belonging to the hotel, the lives and personal property of the guests, and the lives and property of the employees. The specific hazard and its relationship to each of these segments will help determine what protective measures must be taken to provide the desired security.

Regulations Concerning Hazards

In part, the security officer is aided by the existence of laws or statutes that require or prohibit certain acts. There is no discretionary power left to the security officer or to management relative to such laws. If, for example, a fire department regulation limits the number of persons who may occupy a given room, this is a regulation supporting a life-safety code, and failure to comply may result in a fine, legal action or even revocation of a license to operate. Management might like to pack a few more people into that room to gain additional revenue, but they will not risk breaking the law and being punished. Normally, management will make every attempt to comply with legal requirements in order to avoid penalties. (If a security officer becomes involved with an operation in which deliberate infractions of the law are policy and are condoned by management, it is suggested, for his own protection, that he seek employment elsewhere.)

Many of the hazards to be experienced are not covered by statute or other legal decree and must be controlled or regulated by rules promulgated by management. The implementation of these security measures becomes discretionary upon the owner, and the consequences of lack of security may be confined to a financial loss (although the loss may be greater if obvious negligence can be attributed to management).

This presents a serious matter for consideration, and these security measures should be given thorough study as to the degree of hazard present and the possible consequences to life and property. For example, there are no laws on the books to our knowledge indicating what action is to be taken in the event of a bomb threat. The decision to evacuate or not rests with the building owner. This is a decision that should be planned for well in advance, not on the spur of the moment under emotional conditions. Preplanning for all contingencies cannot be over-emphasized, regardless of the number of past incidents.

Perhaps there has never been an armed holdup in the history of a given hotel. That is not to say there never will be one, and plans should be formulated as to what action will be taken in the event of such an incident. Security is a living thing and does not remain fixed. Conditions in the world as well as conditions within the establishment change; personnel change, new hazards arise, new security measures are developed both in concept and in physical equipment. Any security system must keep pace with the changes that are taking place, and it is the security officer's responsibility to suggest the necessary changes and to implement them when approved.

The New Orleans Tragedy

There are also changes taking place in the attitude of the public toward crime as it occurs within the hotel. These changes are mirrored in the courts, in the attitudes of judges and juries as they ponder claims brought against innkeepers. The validity of this statement is apparent in the case of *Dorothy J. Steagall, et al. vs. Civic Center Site Development Company, Inc., and Consolidated Cases,* adjudicated in Federal District Court, New Orleans, Louisiana, early in June, 1975. This case, the principles it raised and the concepts it developed, will be referred to a number of times in later portions of this book.

Briefly, the case involved a claim in excess of $11 million by a number of defendants against the Downtown Howard Johnson's Hotel for an incident in which seven persons were killed and more than twenty wounded by a man who entered the hotel illegally and committed arson as well as murder until he was finally killed by police.

The very important lesson to be learned from this case is that the crime of the street is no longer confined to the street and well may be committed within the hotel. Security officers for years have felt that preventing thefts from guests and from the hotel was their biggest problem, but today they must realize that they must take every step possible to prevent other violent crimes which can and do occur daily in hotels around the world. The mistakes committed in this instance by the owners of the Howard Johnson's Hotel are the same mistakes that innocent and uninformed innkeepers are making today.

Crime is increasing in frequency and severity, the responsibility of management to prevent crime is increasing, and so security must increase though the application of new knowledge, new equipment and an increased awareness of the potential dangers facing us daily. Failure on the part of security will result in additional costly mistakes.

Objective of Security

It cannot be repeated often enough that hotel security is a *preventive* program—the prevention of those hazards that can hurt, injure or destroy lives or property. It is for this purpose and this purpose alone that laws are passed and security measures taken. A security department that can brag about its number of arrests and convictions is not doing its job properly. We are only interested in apprehension if prevention fails. There are no laws or apprehensions involved in natural disasters, for example, so all we can be concerned with is a preventive program designed to minimize loss or damage to life and property when disaster does occur. This is what security is all about.

DELEGATION OF RESPONSIBILITY

A hotel in many ways is similar to a small city in that within its walls may be found restaurants, bars, sleeping rooms, public meeting rooms, variety stores, laundries, mechanical engineering departments, telephone switchboards, garages, entertainment facilities, medical facilities, sales departments, auditing and banking facilities, and protection departments.

Where a city is responsible for supplying municipal services and enforcing rules and regulations as they apply to those living and doing business within the city, one party is responsible for everything that goes on in a hotel. This party is the owner. Whether the owner is an individual, a partnership, a corporation or a government, each is considered a legal entity and is held ultimately responsible for everything that occurs within the hotel and the acts or omission of acts of employees and/or agents. Individuals within the organization may also be held accountable on the basis of their individual responsibility. For example, if an employee should strike a guest in a fit of anger, the injured party would in most cases bring a civil suit for damages against the hotel and the employee as well. Legal responsibility cannot be passed from owner to manager, nor can it be passed from manager to security officer.

The services and facilities available in a hotel are wide and varied, and the owner normally does not become directly involved in the day-to-day management of the property. The owner sets the policy to be followed and places the responsibility for implementing this policy in the hands of a manager. Depending on the size of the property, the manager will delegate certain responsibilities to assistant managers and/or department heads. The relationship between the manager and his department heads is a day-to-day, face-to-face situation, and cooperation between department heads and management as well as among departments is vital to the hotel's success. Failure of one department to carry out its responsibilities in a satisfactory manner can have a serious effect on every other department.

Responsibility for Security

For many years those responsible for security in a hotel were members of one or more departments. In some cases they came under the Service Department, where watchmen, guards, doormen, restroom attendants and house officers were all placed together. In other cases, they might be under the direction of an assistant manager with orders to report not only to the front office manager but to several other department heads.

Over the years, hotel executives have come to realize the importance of security and the extent of its responsibilities. In most large establishments today, security is a department unto itself with the Chief Security Officer as department head and responsible only to the most senior member of management.

This is the ideal situation. However, some establishments do not feel they are sufficiently large to warrant a separate department for security, and the matter is made a collateral duty for some other department head. When this occurs, normally little effort is extended toward pursuing an active security program, as each department or employee is left to formulate security within his own realm, with resultant poor performance. Security is a full-time job, whether it requires one person or many, and those engaged in security should be properly trained, supported completely by management, and reimbursed properly for services rendered.

A difficulty arises in that management cannot see where security produces any income and therefore considers it an expense only. Preventive programs seldom if ever produce income, but they can and do prevent great losses, which management should be equally desirous of accomplishing. Any establishment undertaking the formation or updating of a security department is going to do so with a great deal of caution. Any security officer would do well to walk slowly, but firmly, into such a new set-up. Making big demands for staff, equipment and high salaries will not increase his popularity or chances of success.

Security Job Description and Characteristics

Just who is a security officer and what kind of man is he? What is expected of him and what can he expect in return? A job description of the position might read as follows:

Title: Security Officer (or House Officer, House Detective, etc.)

Duties: Makes rounds of hotel corridors, public rooms and lobbies, observing any unusual or suspicious activities on the part of guests or employees; accompanies credit manager and opens rooms where the latter wishes to examine the baggage and room of a doubtful guest; evicts undesirable guests or loiterers from the hotel; sees that employees do not steal from guests or from the hotel; observes persons entering the hotel and advises room clerks to refuse registration to those known to be of bad character or undesirable for good cause; investigates any accident occurring in the hotel, obtaining evidence to be used in case the hotel is sued; investigates any robberies occurring in the hotel and endeavors to discover the guilty party and recover the stolen goods; assists in the arrest of "wanted" persons in the hotel at the request of law enforcement agencies; ensures compliance with local, state or provincial and federal laws pertaining to any operation within the hotel; writes a complete report of incidents occurring during working hours as well as recommendations for the correction of any hazards or potential "trouble spots"; provides escort service to cashiers when required.

Equipment: Revolver, blackjack, handcuffs, passkey, flashlight, walkie-talkie. (The decision to arm or not to arm shall rest with management. The issue is discussed at length in Chapter 2.)

Working Conditions: Hazards include possible injury from violent or intoxicated persons. Considerable walking required.

Specialized Qualifications: Should be in good health, trained in self-defense. Should possess knowledge of local criminal and civil law, police and fire regulations pertaining to hotels. Should be well-groomed and neat in appearance, possess a pleasing personality, be sober and honest above question.

Desirable Qualifications: Bi-lingual; investigative or law enforcement training.

Related Occupations: Watchman, guard, police officer, fire prevention officer, peace officer, insurance investigator.

It should be pointed out that there is no reason why the position of security officer could not be filled by a female as long as she meets the qualifications. Indeed, there are many times when a woman would be of far greater use than a man, as has been proven in many police departments today where female officers handle juveniles and other females. Therefore, we would point out that all comments made concerning the occupation of security officer are not intended to be limited to one sex.

New Role for Hotel Security

The job description just outlined bears little resemblance to the "house dick" of yesterday as some may remember him or as portrayed in movies, theater or literature. The overstuffed, retired police officer in the dark suit and derby hat, sitting in the lobby behind a newspaper, smoking his cigar, did exist; surprisingly enough, he did serve a purpose in the 1800's and early 1900's. The requirements of the job in those days were much simpler, as were the laws under which society lived. Fewer people traveled and fewer still could afford to stay at hotels. Standing in a hotel lobby, the house detective could easily identify who "belonged" and who did not merely by observing the strangers' attire.

Times have changed as well as fashions, so that today a person's dress is no indication of his ability to pay or his desirability as a guest. The old-time house officer knew that his badge and gun were all the authority he needed to enforce his law as he saw it. With complex legal and ethical issues involving discrimination, civil rights and liberties, the right to privacy, etc., today, the security officer must be educated and rely more on tact and psychology than on force to maintain his authority . . . as is true in all law enforcement.

Perhaps the greatest asset a hotel security officer can have is a pleasing personality and a genuine interest in people that is reflected in his behavior. Surely he must be firm when firmness is required, and in no case can he allow himself to be compromised. He must be inquisitive in nature yet not nosy; he must be friendly yet not familiar; he must be courageous yet not foolhardy; he must be intelligent yet not pretentious; he must be tactful yet not "mushy." Finally, he must be fair and completely honest, yet not "holier-than-thou." Add to these qualifications a knowledge of the daily operations of every department and employee in the hotel. The hotel security officer must be part lawyer, paramedic, clergyman, policeman, investigator, administrator, planner, salesman, judge and jury.

As you can see, the ideal security officer is a special sort of person. The duties and responsibilities of the position cannot and should not be placed in the hands of anyone without these qualifications if the desired results are to be obtained. Again, the investment necessary to secure the proper man to handle the position properly will be well spent by hotel management.

Chapter 2

Security Department Organization

It can be said that, aside from the manager, no other position in the hotel entails as much variety or such a wide scope of activity and responsibility as that of security officer. The difficulty exists that in many cases management is unaware of what a security officer can and should do for the operation, and they have failed to delegate the necessary responsibility to acquire the proper results. It is hoped that this book will be read by management as well as security personnel so that the many possible areas of responsibility will be recognized and the security officer will receive the support and authority he needs to perform to his fullest capacity and ability.

The range of responsibilities of the hotel security officer will be covered in detail in following chapters. How the security officer goes about these duties depends on many factors. Among them are the following considerations:

1. How large a staff will the security department have?
2. What facilities and equipment will be provided for the department?
3. What authority will be given the security officer and what position will he hold in the hotel's operational chain of command?
4. What are the security vulnerabilities of the particular facility? (See Chapter 3.)

THE SECURITY STAFF

Naturally, the number of persons directly involved in security will determine how the security officer will be required to spend his time. If there is only one employee in the security department who must assume all the responsibilities himself, arrangements will have to be made to attend to the most pressing needs on a day-to-day basis. The working hours will have to be adjusted to cover the most hazardous periods. Hotels and motels operate on a 24-hours-a-day, seven-days-a-week basis, and security should be provided at all times. If only one person is employed to provide that security, it is evident that there will be periods of time when no one is in charge. What possible assistance can be provided under such circumstances?

Personnel in the security department may include watchmen, guards, security officers and assistants. Each has a particular role to play in the provision of security for the hotel operation.

Watchmen

Watchmen are usually defined as persons required to make routine scheduled patrols throughout the premises during given periods to ensure the security of the property and to be alert for hazards. They may or may not be required to punch a watchman's clock or some other device designed to record the time and location of their patrols.

The watchman's clock provides a record of the time a given post on the patrol route was inspected. It is used basically to ensure that patrol rounds are being conducted properly. A central supervised system lets the supervisor know immediately when a watchman fails to reach an appointed location on schedule, so that immediate response can be made to investigate the reason.

The use of watchmen may be required by law, and the security officer should determine if this is a requirement in the area where he is employed. In the State of New Jersey, for example, there is a statute on hotel safety which states in part: "Every hotel over two stories in height where the number of guest rooms exceeds twenty, shall be equipped with an automatic fire detecting system or with automatic sprinklers or shall be patrolled nightly between the hours of eleven p.m. and six a.m. by a watchman recording his rounds on an approved watchman's clock or central station supervisory system. The watchman's stations shall be so located that all parts of the building are visited, and records of each watchman's tour shall be kept available for inspection."

If watchmen are required by law, a sufficient number will have to be employed. It must be remembered that these men will be working during night hours when there are few people around, when dangers and hazards can occur more readily. It is necessary to have conscientious, reliable, well-trained persons acting as watchmen.

Watchmen should be provided with uniforms so they are easily recognized as official representatives of the hotel. They should be provided with the necessary clocks or facilities for recording their rounds. The record of rounds accomplished should be checked daily by the security officer to ensure that they are being conducted in the proper manner. Late rounds or missed stations should be discussed with the responsible watchman to determine the cause. In addition, watchmen should be provided with flashlights and such keys as may be required to open or shut prescribed doors, or to gain admittance for inspections. Watchmen should be trained initially and provided with refresher courses in fire fighting, first aid, and the requirements, regulations and duties of the position as set forth by management. It must be made certain that every watchman knows exactly what is to be done in the event of any emergency or upon discovering any hazard.

While many may consider the watchman's primary role one of fire prevention, their value extends further. As they make their rounds through the building, they are constantly watching for any unusual situations or activities. As such, they operate in an anti-crime role. For example, the person leaving via a fire tower at 3:00 a.m. would be highly suspicious and should be detained for questioning. Unlocked doors or open storerooms bear investigation. The watchman might be compared to the police patrolman walking his beat in the city, checking his area throughout the night, making sure all is safe and secure and investigating unusual situations.

Consideration must be given to providing watchmen as well as other security personnel with some form of instant communications so that messages can be sent and received immediately. The watchman might be required to assist in an emergency or to conduct an investigation in a distant part of the building. Without some form of communication, valuable time could be lost attempting to locate him. The watchman desiring to request assistance or report an incident would be required to locate a telephone if he is not equipped with a means of mobile communication.

In some instances paging devices have been used, utilizing either a tone signal which notifies the bearer to go to the nearest telephone for a message, or a one-way unit by which the bearer can receive a spoken message but cannot reply. It is strongly suggested that two-way walkie-talkies be utilized for the most efficient operation.

The watchman should keep a log in which he records any unusual occurrence during his tour of duty. In this manner a written record is maintained of activity for future reference. If hazards are discovered that cannot or need not be taken care of immediately, a notation can be made to be followed up by the security officer during regular working hours. Any serious incident, or one involving additional details, should be reported by the watchman in a formal statement setting forth all pertinent information. In this manner, the security officer reporting for work in the morning has immediate full knowledge of everything that occurred during the night hours. If an assistant security officer is on duty through the night hours, the responsibility for proper reports will be his, to be reviewed by the chief security officer when he reports for work.

Watchmen have a specific job to do—one that is very important to the security of the hotel. The importance of their job should not be underrated and they should be made to understand that importance. Laziness or incompetence should not be tolerated under any circumstances. A watchman should be alert, physically fit and mentally sound, with unquestionable integrity.

Guards

Guards are normally assigned to a specific area or location (unlike the watchman, who patrols various areas) and are responsible for maintaining security and control at that location. The person who controls the employees' service entrance or the delivery entrance, for example, would be a guard. The person who watches a convention display or checks identification or credentials at the entrance to a meeting room is a guard. There are no known laws stating that guards must be employed in hotels. They are used by management to provide security and control. One instance might be where laws permit a fire exit to be locked *if* a guard is posted at the door at all times.

Guards should be in a uniform that will distinguish them from everyone else and will provide them with an air of authority. The uniform is also a morale factor in that it sets the wearer off from the rest of the employees and helps remind him of his duties and responsibilities. Guards, like watchmen, must be trained and have a full and complete understanding of hotel procedures in the event of emergencies. More important, however, is that guards be instructed as to what is required of them in a specific instance.

If they are to control entrance into a meeting room, for example, they must be instructed as to who is permitted to enter and who is to be turned away. Every detail must be covered if the guard is expected to perform efficiently. While guards will probably not be required to exert the physical activity of a watchman, they should be in good health, mentally and physically, make a nice appearance as they deal with the public, and should be honest and reliable. After all, management relies on them to perform security tasks; if the guards are unreliable or untrustworthy, the hotel will have serious problems.

Female Officers

In the opinion of the authors, a female security officer can be invaluable on certain occasions. It may be that the hotel does not wish to have a full-time female security officer, but there should be one or more female employees trained in security work who could be called upon when needed to perform security functions.

It is sometimes preferable to have another female present when dealing with females. If a female calls from her room requesting a security officer, a smart move would be for that officer to be accompanied by a female. Some females do not hesitate to put a man in a very compromising position. If a woman guest becomes intoxicated and must be assisted to her room, it is advisable for a female employee to accompany the security officer. It is not a question of mistrusting the security officer or questioning his ability to handle the situation; rather it is the embarrassing position the woman can create by false charges or improper conduct. In cases of accident, theft or other incidents, a woman complainant often feels more at ease in the presence of another woman. This is not to say that the male security officer should not be present, but he should be accompanied by a woman representative.

CONTRACT SECURITY VS. PROPRIETARY SECURITY

One of the more difficult decisions which has to be made by the hotel owner is whether the services of a security officer or staff are needed on a full-time basis. In a smaller hotel or motel, it is unlikely that the cost of maintaining a permanent security officer or staff will be justifiable on financial grounds, and the manager will usually have to assume the responsibility for security details among his many other tasks. In such a case, even if watchmen were required by law, they would be under the direct control of the manager and would report to him rather than to a security officer *per se.* It may be advisable, however, for the medium-sized establishment to investigate the cost of a security officer and staff in relation to possible reduction of insurance premiums for fire and other risks, and where losses are persistently occurring. It may prove economical under such circumstances to hire a security officer.

Types of Services Available

It may prove helpful to describe the security services which exist and what they can provide. These may be classified into two broad categories: first, the proprietary security force, which is one hired by the user and placed on his payroll as an employee of the hotel; secondly, the contract service provided by a security agency which provides various services at contract rates to anyone wishing to hire them. The contract services are usually subject to some form of controlling legislation which defines their powers and sets standards of operation, while the proprietary forces are usually not so controlled. The services that may be provided by the security agency may include:

1. Provisions for uniformed security personnel at a per-man-per-hour rate.
2. Provision of private investigators who will carry out inquiries which do not fall within the jurisdiction of the police.
3. Provision and installation of intrusion alarm equipment on a rental basis and provision of an answering service for such alarms.
4. Provision of uniformed security patrols and canine patrols.
5. The electronic sweeping of premises to detect eavesdropping devices or other "bugs."
6. The provision of persons to work undercover, particularly in employee theft detection situations.
7. Provision of personnel for transit security duties such as transporting money to a bank for deposit.

Advantages and Disadvantages

There is something to be said for each category as well as drawbacks for each. The advantages of a proprietary force may be summed up as follows:

1. Proprietary force personnel are hotel employees under the complete control of the hotel. They may be assigned to any duties relevant to security.
2. Proprietary personnel become familiar with the hotel, its policies and operations.
3. The hotel has control over who is hired and can set its own standards as to qualifications, ability, education, etc.

The advantages of a contract service may be summed up as follows:

1. The system is probably cheaper, as personnel are hired or contracted for only as needed. If a man is needed for eight hours only, that is all that is contracted for.
2. There is an assurance of personnel being present with no need for the hotel to worry about vacations, sickness or absenteeism.

3. Specialists are available who might not be required on a day-to-day basis.

The potential disadvantages of the proprietary system include:

1. It is more costly. Good personnel must be compensated at a competitive salary with incentives to continued employment.
2. Absences due to sickness, vacations or other causes present a problem. Additional help is required to cover such vacancies, and the salary of the absent person may continue as an added expense.
3. If employees are bonded, this is an added expense to management.
4. Additional expenses will be incurred such as uniform costs, unemployment and workmen's compensation insurance, pension funds, meal allowances, etc.
5. Security personnel may become too familiar with other employees and thereby compromise their security responsibilities.

The disadvantages of a contract service might include:

1. Limitations due to existing laws as to what the security force may or may not do in performance of its duties.
2. Contract personnel are not as familiar with the hotel, its policies or operations.
3. Contract service personnel are not usually well versed in hotel law and hotel security services . . . unless the agency happens to specialize in such institutions, which is not normally the case.

While we have presented a few of the pros and cons of both services, normally it is either the very small hotel or the extremely large operation that will rely solely on one or the other type. The average hotel will use a combination of the two . . . the proprietary force to maintain day-by-day operations and the contract service to provide exceptional services that will be required from time to time.

Common Contract Services

The most common contract services used by hotels today include:

1. Armored car service for the transportation of money to and from the bank. Normally, such a service is relatively inexpensive and results in a reduction in insurance premiums for coverage of lost or stolen money.

2. The use of undercover agents in the suppression of employee stealing. It is difficult and really unfair to ask an employee to become an outright spy on his fellow employees, but an undercover agent can be used with great success. Such an arrangement should be kept very confidential for the agent's safety and in order to ensure results. Only the manager and the person in charge of security should be aware of the arrangement, and it would be just as well if the identity of the agent was unknown even to them. In most cases, the undercover operation should produce some results in two to three weeks. At the end of this time, the operation should be analyzed carefully to determine whether it should be continued. If the agent has not found anything in two or three weeks, chances are he is not going to. He may be tempted to "invent" situations in order to justify his continued employment.

3. Guard services to handle convention displays, meetings, and other special events are usually handled on a contract basis, as the number of persons required will vary greatly and the times they will be needed is also a great variable. Twenty guards may be required for three days and then no more for a month, so it would not be feasible to have such a staff on the hotel payroll.

4. The use of alarm systems on a rental basis is very common and a great protective measure for the hotel. Silent holdup alarms, whether terminating in a central station or a police department, are valuable preventive and protective devices. If such alarms are terminated internally, or if CCTV is used, the alarms and monitors

must be constantly supervised, which will require additional personnel.

The monitoring of alarm systems is normally not too difficult, for most such alarms activate a light and a sound alarm. It is not necessary for the person responsible to constantly watch the annunciator panel. It is only required that someone be in the immediate vicinity constantly to take appropriate action when an alarm is registered.

SECURITY OFFICERS AND ASSISTANTS

If a security officer is provided as part of the proprietary force, a determination will have to be made as to how many assistants will be required. This will depend on management's decision as to what hours it is desirable to have someone directly responsible for security. If there is more than one security officer, one should be designated Chief Security Officer and should be held responsible for assistants and all personnel in the security department. This Chief of Security should be responsible in turn to the *manager* of the hotel and *no other person*. While he may delegate some of his duties and responsibilities to his assistants, he shall be held ultimately responsible for the operations of his department. In the absence of the Chief Security Officer, an assistant shall be designated to assume his responsibilities, in the same manner a vice president steps in to assume the duties of a president in his absence.

Duties of Chief of Security

The duties of the Chief of Security include:

1. To organize his department in such a manner as to fulfill the requirements for security as set forth by management, and to advise management on security matters.
2. To assist the personnel department in securing the proper employees to fill positions in the security department; or, in the event a personnel department does not exist, to hire the most qualified persons possible to fill the available positions.

3. To train or provide for training of all security personnel in the following areas of responsibility:
   - All hotel regulations and all factors affecting the operations of the hotel as they apply to the hotel's stated policy
   - Unarmed defense techniques
   - Fire prevention and safety techniques
   - Basic fire fighting
   - First aid
   - Swimming and life-saving, if a pool or other water hazard is part of the hotel's facilities
   - Preservation of crime scene and evidence
   - Actions, duties and powers where crime is detected
   - Actions in crisis situations
   - Report writing
   - Public relations, psychology
   - Civil and criminal law of the municipality, state, province or country

4. To supervise all activities of security staff to ensure compliance with and proper application of department regulations and hotel policy.
5. To maintain liaison with local law enforcement agencies and other public safety departments.
6. To maintain adequate and complete records of all activities of the security department.
7. To review policies, procedures and instructions on a regular basis to ensure maintenance of the highest level of efficiency and the best possible security, to make recommendations to management when policy changes are required, and to evaluate on a continuing basis the possible threats to security.
8. To instruct all employees in their responsibilities as they apply to security and safety, and to test regularly not only the systems but also the personnel involved in implementing the systems to ensure their proper application and response.
9. To instill in management and employees a feeling of confidence in the security department.
10. Last but not least, to ensure the safety of the persons

and the property of all within the premises by fairly applying hotel regulations, by strict adherence to existing laws, statutes and applicable ordinances, and by anticipating possible and probable hazards and conditions and either correcting them or pre-planning a defense against them.

This is a lot to ask of any person, and to some it may seem an impossible task. In a large hotel with thousands of guests and other members of the public coming and going each day, with hundreds of employees, thousands of bedrooms, miles of hallways, hundreds of closets, storage places and other hidden areas, numerous entrances and exits, how can the security officer do his job properly no matter how many assistants he might have?

Security Consciousness

The answer to that question, we believe, lies in the fact that the security officer cannot do the job alone. Every employee should be security-conscious. Without all of these extra eyes, the security officer's job will never be accomplished properly. This applies not only to guest activities, but also to employee actions. The security officer must develop a "grapevine" so that information is fed to him. This information should be treated in a confidential manner and the informant should be protected. The employees must trust the security officer and they must know that he will not violate that trust. When an employee has performed in such a manner as to warrant special appreciation and thanks, he should receive credit and public thanks, and possibly an appropriate reward. Once employees find that honesty pays and is appreciated, it becomes more difficult for them to steal.

EQUIPMENT FOR SECURITY

Communications

Communications is the lifeblood of a security officer, whether it be in the form of "tips" from security-conscious employees or direct communications by word of mouth, the written word, or some signaling device. Provisions should be made for all security officers to be equipped with some form of instant communications, preferably a two-way radio. No security officer can confine himself to an office and a desk waiting for the telephone to ring to advise him of trouble. Regardless of how many assistants he may have on his own staff or how good his grapevine may be, the security officer must patrol and see things first hand. At the same time, he must be available for immediate needs. This can only be accomplished by some form of communications system.

Coverage and CCTV

The primary need of any security program is coverage and access control. If security personnel could be stationed on every floor of a hotel in such a way that they could observe every guest room, every storeroom, every cashier, every office, every entrance or exit and every working area of the hotel, there would probably be no theft. As can be easily understood, however, this is impossible, but a good security officer who is constantly on the move, checking every place, observing everything, appearing unannounced on no set schedule, will go a long way toward accomplishing the same thing.

The more a security officer "wanders," the easier it is for him to spot something out of place or suspicious. He can spot not only physical changes but changes in the attitude or behavior of employees. If there is a secret to being a successful hotel security officer, it is this very factor—the complete mobility and watchfulness of that officer.

Closed circuit television must be considered as a possibility in the overall security program. In addition to live cameras, dummy cameras have also been employed to act as a deterrent. It is possible to have constant monitoring to detect possible crime situations and operating problems as well, or to provide a photographic record of a crime as it takes place. Both have value, and the cost of the equipment to establish such a system is constantly being reduced by new advances in design and production methods. This cost factor must be equated against the cost of extra manpower to achieve the same coverage, as well as the increase in security and efficiency provided by CCTV operation.

If a constant film record is being made to be used as later

identification of persons entering the area of coverage, there is no need for monitoring. However, if the unit is designed to enable one man to watch a given area constantly so that immediate response may be made to a situation before it develops into something serious, then a person must devote full time to this duty.

It must be borne in mind that one person can watch only so many monitors at one time, and for a limited time only. No person can be expected to watch a group of monitors constantly for eight hours. The tediousness of such a job lowers a man's attention after a period of time. Expecting him to watch the monitors attentively as well as performing other duties (such as dispatching, answering telephones, and checking persons entering the building) is unrealistic and would greatly reduce the value of the system. If the monitor is not going to be watched, its value is highly questionable.

Uniforms

The question of a "police-type" uniform as opposed to civilian attire for security personnel is also one subject to varying opinions. Some feel that seeing a number of uniformed officers on the property is detrimental to the reputation of the hotel. It may look like an armed camp, and the guests may question how safe the hotel is if all these uniformed men are required. On the other hand, guests may appreciate the presence of uniformed officers and feel safer knowing they are on the job.

It must also be remembered that the uniformed officer may serve as a deterrent to the prospective criminal. Some criminals will search out the easy "hit," one where there are no known security officers, rather than attempt a confrontation with a uniformed man. There is no doubt that the uniform assists the officer in establishing his authority in the event of an incident.

Often a compromise on the matter of uniforms for security personnel is established. The security officer, security director, or whatever title is applied, and his assistants may dress in civilian attire while guards, watchmen and other security personnel may be attired in a distinctive uniform.

Firearms

The question of whether to arm security personnel often arises. The answer to this may be simple or complex. In certain areas and in some countries, it is illegal for anyone other than a sworn law enforcement officer to carry firearms. In such a case there is no question—the hotel security officer is not a law enforcement officer and therefore cannot bear arms.

In other areas, the law may not be as restrictive and it may be permissible for hotel security officers—whether they are contract employees or a proprietary force—to be armed. If the law does permit a choice in the matter, law enforcement officials, security consultants and others differ in their opinions, with some favoring arms and others equally opposed.

Management's decision whether to arm the security officer must be made only after careful consideration. A hotel is no place for a "shoot-out." When we consider lobbies filled with innocent people, corridors where guests may step from doorways unexpectedly, the possibility of someone being injured or killed in a shooting incident is a real one. It is also suggested that an armed intruder is more likely to shoot another armed person than an unarmed one. The injury of an innocent bystander by a security officer may result in costly litigation for the hotel.

On the other hand, there are instances where an armed officer might be the answer to prevent additional death and destruction. In the Howard Johnson's case referred to in Chapter 1, the record shows that an armed man was in the building. It was known he had already killed several people. The person acting as the security officer unexpectedly came face to face with the accused, who at that moment was attempting to clear his jammed weapon. The employee was unarmed. Fearing for his life, he turned and ran to escape but was shot in the back by the accused. Had the security officer been armed and trained in the use of his weapon, he might have been able to disarm the accused or, if the accused failed to surrender his weapon, the employee could have shot him to protect his own life. The lives of five additional victims might have been saved, and others might have escaped injury.

Perhaps an incident such as this will happen only once in a

lifetime, but should we not be prepared? More and more crime of a serious nature is being committed today, involving life and death, and it may be that management will feel this added security is worthwhile. If arms are to be used, it must be absolutely certain that those entrusted with this responsibility be properly trained not only in the actual use of the weapon, but also in handling stress situations, so that unnecessary use of the weapon does not result. A person with an uncontrolled temper, or any psychological hang-up, should not be permitted to carry a weapon.

The answer to the question of firearms may lie in the hiring of armed guards from a contract service. To protect the hotel in such a case, a "save harmless" clause should be included in the contract of services to be provided. Such a clause places all responsibility for the acts of the contract employees on the Contractor. The Contractor assumes all liability for his employees, thereby "saving the Innkeeper from any claims brought against him for the misconduct or misdeeds of the contract employee. In the event that the Innkeeper is made party to a civil suit caused by the acts of the contract employee, the Contractor must defend the Innkeeper, and if damages are awarded, the Contractor is liable for said damages."

Certainly, whether a hotel hires contract armed guards or employs its own armed force, those entrusted with firearms must be highly trained and must requalify their marksmanship on a regular basis.

If it is felt that the security officer may be in danger of bodily harm (as is an increasing probability today), the possibility of using non-lethal weapons should be explored. Many of these weapons are very effective and are legal where firearms are not.

ETHICS OF THE SECURITY PROFESSION

It would be impossible to detail minutely how a security officer should perform his job. Each man will have a different approach and each premises will require special handling. On a broad basis, we would offer the following suggestions for consideration. Although most are general in nature, experience has shown that they are very important to a successful security program. For All Security Department Personnel:

1. If a uniform is worn, it should be a complete outfit, clean

and pressed. If a necktie is required, it shall not be worn at "half-mast." Shoes should be shined and metal polished, giving the appearance of a well-groomed, efficient person. Hair should be trimmed and neat. Hands and fingernails should be clean. If civilian clothes are worn, the attire shall be appropriate to the area and type of hotel. The object in being in plain clothes is to appear normal and inconspicuous in a crowd. In an East Coast city, for example, a business suit may be appropriate, while in a West Coast resort area, less formal attire may be the order of the day. Dress, whatever the style, should be clean and neat.

2. No drinking should be permitted while on duty. Friendly guests may invite the security officer to have a drink with them. This should be avoided with a gracious refusal. If a man has had a few drinks before coming to work, every precaution should be taken that his breath does not betray this fact. A security officer with liquor on his breath immediately creates a very bad image.

3. All personal feelings, good or bad, must be kept personal and not allowed to interfere with the performance of duties. Comments on personal appearance, race, color, or ethnic background are out of order. All persons must be treated with the same degree of respect.

4. The most important asset a hotel has to offer is service, and the security officer has many opportunities to be of service. A guest with a problem needs help, not a lecture or a cold shoulder. The problem may not have been the fault of the hotel, but the guest is not interested in whose fault it is. All he wants is someone to help him, and this the security officer should do. The security officer is a top representative of management and the entire hotel may be judged by his actions.

5. Security personnel should accept no gratuities from anyone. If a guest wishes to reward a member of the security staff for services rendered, the employee should graciously refuse. If the guest insists, he should be requested to present the gratuity to the manager in the name of the security officer. Nothing should be accepted from employees, whether it be a drink, food or anything else. Such action, regardless of how innocent, places the officer in a compromising position. In the same respect, the security officer should ask for nothing from an employee, as the same compromising position would be created.

6. The security officer should never threaten legal action or

bodily harm unless intending to carry out the threat if necessary.

7. Any formal complaint made to the police is done by the security officer in the name of the hotel. The officer is acting for the hotel.

8. When investigating an accident, the security officer should never admit any liability on the part of the hotel. He should merely gather the facts in the case, regardless of whether they are helpful or harmful to the hotel, record those facts and leave the decisions on liability to the insurance experts.

9. The security officer should become acquainted with the insurance adjuster responsible for the hotel's liability insurance and have an understanding with him as to when he wants to be called following an accident. Some companies desire to make settlements immediately if the hotel is at fault. In this manner, the injured party does not have time to think about his injury and listen to advice from the people at home who may urge him to increase his claim considerably. In other cases, it may be desirable to wait before offering or making a settlement. This is something that should be discussed by the adjuster and the security officer. The better they know each other, the easier their jobs.

10. At all times a security officer must remain cool, calm and conduct himself in a low key. Such action instills confidence, bespeaks strength and denotes complete control. The screaming, raving officer, flaunting his authority, creates problems for himself and his employer.

11. The security officer should never break a confidence. He will be party to confidential information regarding the hotel, the guests and employees. This information must remain confidential at all times.

12. If the security officer deals fairly with the press, in most cases it will deal fairly with the hotel. The last thing the hotel desires is bad publicity, but news is news and the paper will print what they feel is of interest to the public. If the security officer refuses to cooperate, the story that appears may be blown out of proportion. If the security officer does not desire to make a statement, the reporter should be directed to the manager.

13. Off-duty security officers should stay away from the hotel. It is better in most cases if employees do not make use of the facilities of the hotel where they are employed. Such action again can place all parties in a compromising position.

14. If the room of a female guest must be searched, a woman employee should be in attendance.

15. Accurate and complete records should be kept of all incidents. Every investigation should be as thorough as possible, with names and addresses of all witnesses. Often in liability cases, court appearances may not result until months or years later, when the incident has all but been forgotten by the officer. The records made at the time of the incident will be all the officer has to refer to, so they must be as complete as possible.

16. The security officer should not hesitate to request assistance in solving problems. No one knows everything. The help of legal counsel, law enforcement agencies, fire officials, insurance experts, etc., can make the job much easier.

17. If a potentially troublesome group or person must be approached and some action is going to be required, the plain-clothes security officer should have a uniformed person, whether it be a watchman, guard or police officer, accompany him. Not only does this provide him with a witness, but the appearance of a uniform might prevent violence.

18. If first aid must be administered, only that necessary to protect and sustain human life should be provided. Competent medical assistance should be obtained as soon as possible. The security officer should not prescribe for anyone or allow an injured party to depart unattended. The handling of all types of accidents should be discussed with the hotel's insurance representatives. In many cases, insurance companies will want the victim of any accident to be examined by a physician immediately to prevent an exaggerated claim at a later date. Whatever the insurance company desires should determine the action the officer will take.

19. The security officer should not become socially involved with any guest of the hotel. A friendly, pleasant attitude is very desirable; however, the relationship should extend no further.

20. The security officer should never loan money to an employee or borrow money from an employee.

21. The seniority of an employee or his status in the hotel organization should not intimidate the security officer. Every employee and guest is entitled to the same treatment and should be subject to the same controls. All actions should be based on facts. Personalities should not enter into any decisions on the part of the officer.

22. The security officer should expect no more of his staff or other employees of the hotel than he expects of himself. He must set an example by his conduct, or his position as a leader will be seriously challenged.

Finally, the best advice we can give a security officer is to keep his eyes and ears open and his mouth shut, unless he has something important to say. He should perform according to hotel policy and use common sense. Regulations are formulated as guidelines. Each incident will present a different set of circumstances, and no rules can be formulated to cover every possible incident. Knowing the hotel's policy and the intent of the regulations, however, the security officer should act within those guidelines. He should remember always that his reputation and the reputation of the hotel are at stake, and act accordingly.

Chapter 3

Basic Premise Protection Considerations

The hotel premises must be capable of being made physically secure, particularly at night. The term "physically secure" suggests making it as difficult as possible for unauthorized persons to gain entry unobserved or without the use of force or breaking in in some manner. Physical security also calls for providing some means whereby guests may secure their rooms. Service and supply areas should be secured when unattended to prevent unauthorized entry either by those already in the hotel as guests or employees, or by intruders from outside.

Each hotel or motel will require different physical security measures, since each will vary widely in physical layout, size, location, etc. The objectives to be attained are more or less constant, however, and can be summed up as follows:

1. Security of the perimeter of the premises from clandestine entry for an unlawful purpose.
2. Security of guests' rooms.
3. Security of unattended supply and service areas.

SURVEY AND EVALUATION

The implementation of these objectives will vary greatly depending on local conditions and therefore must come about as a result of a complete security survey and evaluation of the local situation. Many factors must be considered, including the following:

1. Where is the hotel located? Is it an urban or rural area?
2. What police services are available? What is the response time?
3. Is the hotel large or small?
4. Are permanent staff on duty at night?
5. What class of clientele usually frequents the hotel?
6. Is it expected that guests will deposit much high value property with the staff for safekeeping?
7. What is the value of cash, alcoholic beverages, food and other goods normally kept on the premises?
8. Is there an arrangement to deposit cash receipts at a bank at the end of each day? Must large sums of money be kept on the premises overnight?
9. What are the insurance factors? Does the hotel qualify for the Innkeepers Liability Act? What losses are covered in regard to theft from the hotel or from a guest?
10. Are the employees honest and reliable?
11. Are those handling money or valuable merchandise in quantity required to be bonded?
12. Is there a security staff in the hotel? If so, is the staff properly instructed, assigned and being used to the greatest advantage?
13. What is the construction of the hotel . . . old or new, more than one floor, more than one building, etc.?
14. Are fire exits required by law to allow emergency exit but prevent casual entry?

While some of these factors appear obvious, a few comments on each are worthwhile.

Location of Hotel

While the hotel's location will not change over the years, the immediate neighborhood might well change. The problems faced by the large hotel located in the center of a busy city will differ from those of the mountain retreat fifteen miles from the nearest town, or those of the motel on an open highway. What is of concern is the type of people around the hotel and how easily they can reach the property. The greater the density of population, the higher the crime rate and the greater the precautions that must be taken for physical security.

Police Protection

The initial responsibility is naturally with management to provide its own protection; however, the location of the hotel will determine the number of police patrols in the area that will be available for immediate assistance. In a busy city it is difficult for even the most alert police patrol to spot a suspicious incident around the perimeter of a large hotel, but there are times when a passing patrol can and does investigate such situations. When trouble does occur, the response time is also important. A silent alarm system will not be very effective if the agency responding is five miles away and there is only one officer on duty at night. The amount of protection needed within the hotel will be related in part to the amount of assistance that can be secured from outside law enforcement agencies.

Size of Hotel

This factor is obvious; anyone can understand that one man can only cover so much territory. A multi-story building with numerous entrances or a complex of buildings spread over a large area presents a far more difficult problem than a one-story building, compact, with a minimum of entrances. A larger building does not necessarily mean a more difficult situation; problems are caused by the number of entrances and the layout of the building itself.

Available Staff

Almost every hotel and motel is open for business 24 hours per day; however, most operate with a full complement only 16 hours a day. During the remaining eight hours, a much reduced staff, consisting mostly of cleaners, auditors and other service personnel, is on duty. Activity within the hotel during these late night hours is greatly reduced and an unauthorized person is easier to spot . . . but there are fewer eyes to spot him. One person can see or do only so much, especially when he has other duties to perform during these hours. Most stealing is done under cover of night, so the question of *available* staff is important.

Clientele

As mentioned previously, close observation of the hotel's clientele was a reliable method years ago of determining who belonged and who did not. While this is not as true today, certain hotels have distinctive "character" and attract certain types of people. Some cater to the elderly or the family trade; they may be relatively low in price to attract this type of clientele. Other hotels have a reputation for catering to the wealthy, and as sugar draws the flies, so money and jewelry may draw the thief.

The situation is far more difficult today than it was years ago, as our economy does not have the great differences in wealth that once existed. More people can afford the fine things in life and there is not as much segregation when it comes to hotel accommodations. On the other hand, if the hotel caters to a young crowd and permits illegal acts, such as the use of drugs, to go unnoticed, they can be sure that sooner or later trouble will develop. While the type of clientele is important in security considerations, it is only the extremes that are of great concern.

Value of Property to be Protected

This is where management sometimes loses sight of why security is necessary. In general the hotel is obligated to protect the guest and his belongings (although this obligation may be limited by statute, as we shall see later). In addition, the real, fixed and liquid assets of the hotel . . . the food, beverages, supplies, equipment and cash, to mention a few . . . are worth money. The loss of any of these could cause financial disaster. The security measures taken must depend on the value of the material or items to be protected. There is no need to put a lock on a room door if there is nothing in that room. Conversely, it is foolhardy not to secure a building containing thousands of dollars worth of goods and materials. It boils down to the question, just how much is the hotel willing to spend to protect what it has from loss?

Employee Theft

The question of whether an employee is honest is one that no one has been able to answer correctly 100% of the time. Past records may be an indication of what can be expected, but this is no certainty. Some employees have been known to be honest for many years and suddenly "go bad."

It has been pointed out that many people steal only because the opportunity to do so was present and they were able to get away with it. Without the opportunity and without the temptation, they would never steal. The job of security is to remove the opportunity. In dealing with employees, it makes little difference what kind of hotel it is, where it is located, how big it is, how long the employee has been on the job, how many are employed. A human being, if he has the opportunity to steal and decides to do so, will not be affected by these factors. The most difficult security problem is handling people, whether they are employees, guests or outsiders, and knowing what to expect from each person.

Employee Safety

Security is an all-encompassing word; while some may wish to separate security and safety, we believe such a separation cannot be made. The protection of life and property from injury is just as much a part of security as protecting items from theft or destruction. Security officers, therefore, must be aware of potential hazards to the health and welfare of any person within the hotel. There are a number of statutes that govern working conditions and methods of operation as they pertain to the employees of a hotel. In the United States these include the Workman's Compensation Act and the Occupational Safety and Health Act, the full implications of which are not known at this time. In Canada, there is the Industrial Safety Act, as well as others. To attempt to define the requirements of these acts would require another entire publication. Suffice it to say that the security officer should determine what regulations in this field he must operate under and should learn the contents of these acts.

Security Personnel

Physical security considerations must include what personnel are available for security responsibilities. The security staff might be untrained, unorganized and not properly assigned, but at least they constitute a starting point . . . in contrast to a situation where no manpower exists for security. Using manpower in an efficient manner is a very important factor in a physical security plan.

Construction of the Hotel

This is an important factor in the overall survey of security needs, as it may point out just how vulnerable the hotel is to security breaches. For example, an old hotel may have old doors that no longer fit properly and locks that no longer hold securely. A hard lunge against the door might force it to open easily, while a strong door with a good lock in a modern building would resist such treatment.

If the cost of replacing all old doors and locks is out of the question, a serious problem exists and must be planned for accordingly. Perhaps there is no solution to the problem, but security and management must be aware of the situation. This is not to say that older hotels are necessarily faced with greater risks and are more likely to be victims of security breaches than newer hotels; however, some older buildings do present problems that are not encountered in more modern construction.

Laws Affecting Hotel Rights and Duties

In the English-speaking world, wherever hotels exist, there are laws that govern their operations. These laws may be contained in one statute or in a collection of statutes. The names by which they are referred to may differ and the provisions may differ from state to state and from province to province. Basically they are similar and their purpose is to outline the rights, duties and responsibilities of innkeepers in respect to the property of guests.

Many regional hotel associations have compiled the appropriate laws and published them for the convenience of their members. It would be well for every security officer and hotel manager to contact his local association and secure such a publication if it exists.

It is important to realize that there are two kinds of liability to which an innkeeper is subject. The first is obvious and implies that he is liable if he himself is in some way negligent in carrying out his obligations or fails to carry them out. Secondly, he is open to what is known as "vicarious liability." This means that he will be liable for the actions or neglect of his servants or persons under his control . . . even if he had no knowledge of what they were doing at the time. This poses the obvious requirement for special care in hiring reliable employees and ensuring that they are properly trained in their duties and responsibilities. An example of such liability would occur where a hotel was charged with serving alcoholic beverages to a minor contrary to law. It would make no difference that the innkeeper himself was not present at the time the infraction took place.

Briefly, these statutes or acts include a definition of what constitutes a hotel (see Chapter 1); duty to maintain a register; duty to receive guests; civil rights considerations; ejectment of guests or others under certain conditions; Innkeepers Liability for property on the premises belonging to guests and the monetary limitations of that liability; liability for loss by fire or force; innkeeper's duty to protect guests from personal injury; fraud and bad check laws; the innkeeper's lien and methods of foreclosure; provisions for providing safekeeping facilities; and such other laws pertinent to hotels. It is vital that management and security have a thorough knowledge of these laws in order to provide the necessary security to fulfill their responsibilities.

Summary

Once a security survey has been completed and the problems and requirements of security are understood, the hotel security department can then act effectively. The following advantages can be realized:

1. For a reasonable outlay, the risk of loss can be greatly reduced.
2. The risk of claims by guests in respect to stolen property and personal damage may be lessened.

3. Insurance premiums may be less costly.
4. The reputation and good name of the hotel will be protected.

In the chapters that follow it will be our intent to discuss each major phase of the hotel operation in an attempt to point out some of the more common security problems and offer some practical solutions. It must be pointed out again that a given solution may not be successful in every instance, and the ingenuity of the security officer involved is going to play an important part in solving the problem.

Chapter 4

Persons Entering
the Premises

A hotel is considered a quasi-public building, available to anyone having proper business therein. Persons entering the building will usually fall into one of the following classifications:

1. A guest
2. A visitor of a guest
3. An invited guest of management but not a guest of the hotel in the strict legal sense
4. An employee
5. An outside contractor
6. A trespasser or other undesirable person.

The rights of each type of person differ, and the obligations of management to each differ. The classification a person falls into will be determined basically by his motive for entering the building. Normally, a person does not declare his purpose when passing through the front door of a hotel, and this determination must be made later. However, a preliminary screening can be made at every entrance where a person is in attendance, whether it be a doorman, watchman, timekeeper or some other representative of management. Admittance can be denied at this point to certain classes of people.

DENYING ENTRANCE TO UNDESIRABLE PERSONS

Intoxicated Persons

An intoxicated person is considered undesirable and can be denied entrance to a hotel. It will sometimes be obvious by such a person's appearance that he is not a guest of the hotel. Such a person should be stopped by the doorman and sent on his way. If he fails to cooperate and leave the area, the police should be called to remove him. Public drunkenness in most places is a minor offense, to be handled by the police.

The occasion may arise when a guest of the hotel returns from a night on the town in an intoxicated state. He may be brought to the hotel door in a taxi, by a friend, or even by the police. If there is any doubt, he should be asked whether he is a guest of the hotel. Does he have a key in his possession? Does the registration desk list him as a guest? If he is a bona fide guest, he should be escorted to his room as quickly and discreetly as possible.

If an intoxicated person states that he wants to visit a friend who is a guest in the hotel, he should be denied admittance. As a courtesy, a call might be placed to the guest advising that this person was present and desired to visit. If the guest wants to see the intoxicated visitor, he must be made to understand that he will be responsible for his friend, and that if there is any disturbance, the visitor will be asked to leave. While this is not a legal obligation on the part of the hotel, it is a good public relations move and may prevent hard feelings that could lead to a civil suit later.

An intoxicated person entering the hotel for the purpose of dining or obtaining additional beverage should be turned away in most cases. If he is in the company of others who are not intoxicated, he might be permitted to enter. Good judgment and tact are necessary in making such decisions.

Most employees and outside contractors enter the building through a separate service entrance. No one under the influence of liquor should be permitted to enter. An intoxicated employee can be a great hazard to management, and every attempt should be made to keep such a person off the premises. If an employee is not permitted to enter the building due to intoxication, his department head should be notified immediately so that steps can be taken to cover his job.

Prostitutes

Like the sneak thief or fraud artist, the prostitute does not carry a sign stating her occupation. Normally, the only opportunity a doorman will have to stop a prostitute from entering the hotel is if she is a known frequenter who has been warned or ordered previously to stay away from the premises.

Regardless of how one feels about prostitution personally, this is a matter where management must set a policy for the security officer to follow. A typical procedure is as follows: If a man escorts a "lady" into the hotel, no questions are asked as long as they do not bother anyone else or cause any disturbance. If, however, she later attempts to solicit additional business in the hotel by knocking on guest room doors or approaching men in the bars, restaurants or other public spaces, she should be asked to leave.

The case may occur where a prostitute checks into the hotel and uses her room to conduct her business with other guests or with outsiders. This is in violation of the law and could subject the hotel to the charge of running a disorderly house. The fact that a person becomes a guest of a hotel and receives a room for lodging does not give that person the right to use the room for illegal activities. In such a case, it might be well to request the assistance of the local vice squad, if one is available, to establish proof that the woman is a prostitute, either by a previous record or through surveillance of her activities. Accusing a woman of such activities is a serious matter and could result in legal action against the hotel. Whether the hotel is right or wrong in its accusation, the publicity created by the incident is not favorable. If the problem does arise, it is best to allow the police to handle the matter.

One of the most serious problems that can occur is a call-girl operation run by hotel employees. Bellmen, room clerks and others have been known to have girls available to fill requests from male guests. A call to the proper person requesting "company" or "a little excitement" results in the appearance of a companion. The money paid returns to the operator of the system. Such an operation can do nothing but harm the hotel and should be stopped at all costs. Even though the employees are acting on their own, the hotel is responsible for their actions because they are employees; as such the hotel could be charged with operating a disorderly house or a house of ill repute.

In short, if a guest desires to bring a prostitute into the hotel, the hotel will not object as long as there is no disturbance or soliciting of other guests. However, the hotel will in no way contribute to or assist in promoting this age-old art.

Minors

Certain minors may have a legitimate reason for entering a hotel. If there is any doubt as to their motives, they can be stopped and questioned. Quite often, however, it is obvious that the minor has no business being in the hotel, and he can be stopped right at the front door by a doorman. An example might be juveniles who shine shoes along the street. It is not unusual for them to walk into a hotel and enter the lobby or bars soliciting business. Such behavior does not enhance the image of the hotel.

A minor entering a bar and requesting alcoholic beverages presents a serious problem to management. This subject will be covered more fully in Chapter 8. Needless to say, any act on the part of the hotel which would violate existing law should be avoided at all costs.

Other Undesirable Persons

The presence in a hotel of undesirable persons such as thieves, fraud artists, bookmakers, gamblers, card sharks, etc., will probably not be known until a complaint is received. If an undesirable person is known to the hotel and has been previously convicted or ordered to stay away from the premises, he can be stopped at the door. If a person in this classification is apprehended on the premises and is not a guest, he can be requested to leave the premises immediately or he can be held for the authorities if the hotel desires to prosecute.

Bookmakers and card sharks may be hotel employees who involve other employees by starting card or crap games in locker rooms, or writing numbers on the premises. It should be a firm policy of management that there will be no gambling on the premises by employees. Anyone found engaging in such activity should be subject to discharge. When employees are on the premises they are supposed to be engaged in their job; if they are not working, they should leave.

Trespass Warning Forms

Some hotels have found it useful to print a Trespass Warning form to be issued to undesirable persons such as prostitutes, gamblers, etc., who frequent the hotel. The warning form serves as written notice to the party that he or she is not to return to the hotel, and that violation of the warning will subject the person to arrest and prosecution by the hotel for trespassing. The form is signed by the ejected person as well as the security officer. It includes a physical description of the subject and leaves space for remarks (location of offense, etc.).

If a person who has previously received a Trespass Warning re-enters the hotel, he or she may be placed under citizen's arrest by a security officer. A Trespass Report form is filled out, including details of the incident, and is signed by the arresting officer and by the party into whose custody the trespasser is released (police, parent, guardian, other).

In some hotel security departments, photographs of prostitutes or other undesirables known to frequent the hotel are kept on file to facilitate identification by security officers if they re-enter the hotel.

DUTY TO RECEIVE GUESTS

As has been pointed out, a hotel keeper is bound under the common law to furnish lodging and entertainment, to the extent of his accommodations, to all suitable persons who apply. He cannot, if he has rooms available, arbitrarily refuse to receive as a guest anyone who is willing to pay the reasonable charges for such accommodations. A hotelkeeper, however, is not compelled to receive *everyone;* he may refuse to accept those undesirable persons just discussed as well as any person deemed to be filthy, profane, behaving indecently or improperly, or one suffering from contagious or communicable diseases.

Also, generally speaking, a person who is not a guest has no legal right to enter and remain in a hotel against the will of the innkeeper. The public rooms of the hotel are maintained for the convenience of guests and patrons and those who have legitimate business with them. Guests' visitors are admitted, not because of any duty which the innkeeper owes to the visitor, but because of the duty which he owes to the guest. When idlers, salesmen or canvassers enter and remain in the lobby and public rooms, the innkeeper is within his rights in requesting them to depart. If they refuse to do so, they may be ejected with the use of as much force as reasonably necessary.

One authority on this subject has stated: "When persons enter a hotel or inn, not as guests, but intent on pleasure or profit, to be derived from intercourse with its inmates, they are there, not by rights, but under an implied license that the landlord may revoke at any time; because barring the limitation imposed by holding out inducements to the public to seek accommodations at his inn, the proprietor occupies it as his dwelling house, from which he may expel all who have not acquired rights, growing out of the relation of guests." *(14 R.C.L. 573.)*

Who Is A Guest?

No person can make himself a guest without the innkeeper's assent. He must present himself to the innkeeper or his agent or servant, request accommodations and give the innkeeper an opportunity to receive or reject him. There is no formal contract in the guest-host relationship. The exact moment a person becomes a guest may differ in different states or provinces. In some instances, the relationship may be established when the guest's baggage is delivered to the hotel a reasonable time prior to the guest's arrival. Others have held that the relationship comes into existence when the key to the guest room is delivered to the guest. Although maintaining a guest register is required by law in most areas, the signing or not signing of the register does not affect the guest-innkeeper relationship.

Persons Attending Special Events

People who enter a hotel to attend meetings, banquets, dances or other events are not guests of the hotel in the legal sense of the word; they are not registered and have not taken room accommodations. They are in the same class as those who enter the inn to patronize the restaurant or bar. The innkeeper in effect has extended an open invitation to these people to enter; however, he also has the right to withdraw this invitation at his own discretion.

Persons entering an inn should do so with a specific purpose in mind. The security officer has the right (and duty, as far as the hotel is concerned) to question the person as to his business. The hotel's facilities are for the use of its guests. If the public is invited to patronize certain areas, such as bars, restaurants and stores, this does not mean that other areas are also available for the general public. The lobby is not a public sitting room where any person may linger and rest. Sleeping floors and rooms are reserved for guests. Recreation areas are for the use of guests, as are sun decks, observation towers, and any other areas the innkeeper so designates.

Ejection of Guests or Others

As we have pointed out, the innkeeper has the right to promulgate reasonable rules governing the use and enjoyment of the accommodations in his hotel. When any such rule is violated by a guest, he should be informed of the rule and requested to act accordingly. If after such request the guest willfully persists in violating the rule, the innkeeper is within his rights in ejecting the offender.

In the case of the non-guest, the innkeeper may withdraw his permission to be on the premises at will and may request the person to leave at once. Failure to comply with the innkeeper's request within a reasonable time gives the innkeeper the right to use as much force as reasonably necessary to make the eviction.

Anytime an eviction takes place and force must be used, the law clearly states that such force shall be only that amount that is reasonably necessary. Every opportunity should be given a person to comply with the innkeeper's request before force is applied. Ejecting a guest can cause poor public relations and bad publicity and should be avoided if possible; however, there will be times when such action is necessary. It should be accomplished as quickly, carefully and discreetly as possible. (The removing of a disabled person presents special hazards and should be accomplished with great tact and with the assistance of a doctor, if necessary.)

The hotelkeeper may also eject a guest for non-payment of his bill. This right of ejectment exists even where the relationship may be that of lodger or boarder rather than the technical relationship of a guest. It should be noted, however, that such right of summary ejectment does not exist where the legal relationship is that of a tenant. A tenant may be ejected only after summary proceedings have been instituted in accordance with the provisions of the applicable statutes.

POLICE COOPERATION

In most instances, the police are more than willing to cooperate with the hotel, especially where a law has been violated. While they are willing to assist in ejecting undesirable persons, they do not like to be placed in the position of being the official "bouncer" of the hotel.

If the hotel desires to press charges against an offender, the police will take the accused into custody pending an official complaint registered by the innkeeper. Such complaints are usually made by the security officer, signed by him as an agent of the hotel. The police, however, should not be called upon to make a routine ejection unless the matter gets out of control or the person being ejected has continually violated hotel rules or continues to return after having ejected.

Close cooperation with the police is a vital part of a security officer's program; however, the police should not be required to do the security officer's work for him. Under the statutes in many states, the police have no right to enter a hotel without the innkeeper's permission or a properly prepared warrant (except in pursuit of a person charged or suspected of a serious offense). It can be seen that cooperation is necessary on both sides between the police and management.

There will be times when the police will be called upon to render substantial assistance, such as in civil disorders or mass actions. This matter will be covered in Chapter 16.

Chapter 5

The Guest Room

The innkeeper has the right to assign a particular room to a guest and retains the right to make a room change. The guest, on the other hand, has the right to expect that the room assigned is for his own personal use and that the innkeeper will respect his privacy. A leading court case has stated: "A hotelkeeper has at all reasonable times and for the proper purposes, the right to access to and control over every part of his hotel even though separate parts thereof may be occupied by guests . . . but, his right of entry into the room of a guest must be exercised with due regard to the occasion and at such times and in such manner as are consistent with the rights of a guest." *(DeWolf v. Ford, 193 N.Y. 397.)*

RESPONSIBILITY FOR LOST PROPERTY

At common law the hotelkeeper was held responsible for the loss of whatever personal property the guest brought into the hotel precincts, including animals, wearing apparel, jewelry, baggage, money and valuables. He was an absolute insurer and was excused only if loss occurred through an act of God, an act of war, or because of the guest's negligence.

Liability Statutes

Most states and provinces have modified the common law by limiting the liability for various classes of property and by permitting the innkeeper to require guests to deposit valuables in the hotel's safe. It has been held that these statutes are to be constructed not so much as limiting the hotelkeeper's liability, as charging the guest with negligence in case he does not avail himself of the protection offered. The statutes make it clear that notices in reference to the safekeeping of valuables should be posted in a conspicuous place and manner. The statutes may provide that such notices be posted in elevators, at elevator landings, and in public rooms, or it may be required that a notice be posted in each guest room. A notice on the hotel register is not considered sufficient.

If a guest tenders his valuables to the proper agent of the hotel and they are refused, or if the innkeeper waives the requirement that the valuables be deposited, the proprietor will be held liable for their loss.

Once proper notice has been given requiring valuables to be placed with the hotel for safekeeping, and the guest complies, the hotel's liability is limited if a loss occurs unless the loss was due to negligence on the part of the hotel's agent or servant. The amount of the liability differs from state to state and province to province.

Proceeding one step further, the question arises of the innkeeper's liability for loss of a guest's personal belongings other than valuables—clothing, baggage, etc.—from the guest room. The statutes covering this matter vary considerably. In general, the innkeeper is not held liable, or his liability is limited to a given dollar value, unless it can be shown that the loss was due to the negligence of the innkeeper or his servants or agents. The burden of proof that no negligence occurred rests with the innkeeper.

Losses from Other Than Guest Room

In the case of loss of a guest's property from some place other than the guest room, where it was not specially entrusted to the proprietor, in general there is no liability on the part of the proprietor. If an article is entrusted to the proprietor or his agent for safekeeping and is lost, the statute designates the extent of liability. For example, if a guest leaves a package in the hotel lobby and the package disappears, the hotel is not liable for this loss no matter what the value. If, on the other hand, the guest checks his coat with an attendant at a hotel restaurant, receives a claim check, and the coat is missing when he attempts to claim it, the hotel is liable to the extent allowed under the statute.

The statutes are clear in every case as to the hotel's liability relative to the guest or to a tenant or boarder. It is strongly recommended that each security officer make himself aware of the statutes that apply in his state or province. (See Chapter 18 for suggested sources of information about hotel law.)

Hotel's Reputation at Stake

Even though the hotel is protected to a degree from claims for losses, nothing hurts a hotel's reputation more than a series of losses from guest rooms. Word of such condition soon spreads, and the guests fear not only for their property but for their lives. Years ago, most thefts from hotel rooms occurred in the absence of the guest. An illegal entry was made by some means, property was removed, and the thief departed. Seldom if ever did the thief carry any weapons, as the difference between robbery or burglary and *armed* robbery could amount to many years in prison. Today, however, we are often faced with armed robbery. Thefts take place at any time of the day or night, whether the occupant is in the room or not. In addition, other crimes, such as rape, arson, or murder, may be committed in the hotel. Regardless of what protection is required by law, every effort should be made to prevent such occurrences for the good reputation of the hotel.

PROTECTION OF DOORS AND WINDOWS

Doors

Naturally, the easiest way to enter any room is through the door. Therefore our first concern must be to provide a door that will delay entry considerably. The authors have witnessed very few cases where a door to a guest room was actually broken to gain admittance; it is not impossible, however. A hollow core door or one with light plywood panels could be broken easily to gain entry. Doors with poor-fitting hardware, or with the hinge bolts accessible to intruders, are dangerous and should be replaced. Where the aesthetic value is of small concern, strong metal doors should be considered. (These thoughts should be borne in mind when considering any doors in the building, not only those on guest rooms.)

In a guest room, there may be additional doors to adjoining rooms or leading to balconies or outside porches. In some motels, the entrance door may open directly off a street, private balcony or an outside common walkway. Each of these situations presents a different problem.

Connecting doors between rooms should be kept locked at all times unless the guests request that they be opened. Some parties, especially families, will have adjoining rooms and want these doors open. Locks, or at least a good hook-and-eye arrangement or door chain, should be provided on both sides of the door. Even though a guest may unlock or unfasten the door on his side, he cannot unlock the door on the opposite side unless he enters the other room. When rooming guests, bellmen should make sure communicating doors are locked securely.

Doors which are not designed to be the primary means of entering a room, whether they be flush, French, sliding glass or whatever, should be provided with locks that are controlled from the inside only. If glass doors are used, they should be provided with non-transparent drapes. In some cases, one-way glass has been used, but this does not eliminate the desirability of having drapes cover these windows or doors.

Master Key Systems

Locks and keys comprise one of the biggest problems facing management and the security officer. A lock is only as good as the control of the key to that lock. There are many new systems on the market today to replace the old tumbler lock or the mortise lock; however, the key control problem still exists since access must be provided to maids and other personnel.

A typical system of locks and keys in a hotel is as follows. There are a number of master keys which will open all guest room doors. These keys are usually in the hands of the manager, his assistants, the security officer, certain maintenance personnel, and the executive housekeeper and his assistants. A very close accounting should be made of these keys and the loss of one should be reported to the security officer immediately. If a key is in any way damaged or becomes worn, it should be destroyed beyond recognition. Only an authorized locksmith or the manufacturer of the lock should be permitted to make duplicate master keys.

In some cases there is also what is known as a "lockout" key. There should be only one or two of these at most, and they should be in the possession of the manager or the credit manager. If a guest has not paid his bill upon demand or if the room must be secured for some other reason, the room is locked with this key. It then cannot be opened by any other key, even a master, and is therefore as secure as possible.

In addition to the grand master keys, there are usually floor masters which will unlock all the doors on a given floor. These are used by maids, housemen or inspectresses assigned to a given floor. The floor master is good only for the designated floor.

Finally there are the individual room keys which are used by the guests. As one can readily see, key control becomes a major problem from every aspect.

Key Control Problems

Keys to guest rooms are normally handed out at the front desk or by a key clerk. When the guest is first assigned a room, a key is presented to him. He may keep this key in his possession for the duration of his stay at the hotel, or he may return it to the desk when he leaves the room and pick it up later when he returns. Any person requesting a key from the desk should be asked to properly identify himself. A request such as "May I have the key to room 917, please?" is not sufficient. The clerk should ask the name of the person making the request and check his name against the hotel register to be certain that person is the occupant of the room. In some cases, it is advisable to ask the address of the person as well. It is possible a thief would know the room number and name of the guest, but he would probably not know the guest's address unless he had done considerable research.

Keys are kept at the desk for the use of the guests should not be left unattended or accessible to anyone reaching over the desk. As keys will sometimes be lost, a reserve supply must be kept for immediate replacement. These reserve keys should be kept in a secure place and should not be accessible to unauthorized persons.

Guests will lose keys or carry them away with them. Every opportunity should be taken to remind guests to turn in their keys upon departure. A polite question at the time the bill is being paid, a question as they depart from the hotel, a notice over the departure door, may help to remind the forgetful guest. Many hotels attach a small tag to their keys indicating that if the key is removed unintentionally from the premises, the finder may drop it in a mail box and it will be returned, with postage paid by the hotel. This system has been effective, but many establishments have made the mistake of placing the hotel's name on this tag together with the address. Anyone finding that key knows exactly what hotel room it will open. It is far better to show only a post office box number and the name of the city. In this manner, the hotel gets the key back and no one except the post office department knows what hotel is involved.

Obviously, no keys should be left lying around unattended. If they are not in the immediate possession of some person, they should be in a secure location. Maids and others using master keys in their work should carry them firmly attached to a key strap worn around the waist. They should not be hung from the maid's cart, nor should they be left in a door as the maid works in a room. No bedroom door should be opened for a guest by the maid unless the guest is personally known to her. It is very easy for a thief to approach a maid and state that he forgot his key, or his wife has the key, and would the maid mind opening his bedroom door? Such an action would be negligence on the part of the employee if the person was not the occupant of that room.

Keys not in use should be kept in a secure location and distributed only by authorized persons who will keep a record of any keys given out. All of this may seem tedious and time-consuming, but key control is a preventive measure that gives at least some additional security.

Naturally, a problem occurs when a guest deliberately keeps a key to a room with the intention of returning at a later date. He could then enter the hotel at his leisure and place a call to the room from a lobby telephone. If there is no answer, he can enter the room, take any valuables he desires and leave. If someone answers his call, he asks for a certain person to make an excuse for calling, and bides his time until the occupant leaves the room. Many hotel thieves when apprehended are found to have a number of hotel keys in their pockets.

Potentially far more dangerous is the dishonest employee in possession of a master key or sub-master key. Such keys should be issued daily to those employees requiring them and accounted for at the end of the shift of duty. A written record should be kept of such issues, and any losses should be reported at once to the security department and investigated immediately. This does not solve the problem completely, as an impression of a key could be made while the employee is on duty and a copy made at a later date. The best protection against such occurrences is to have honest, reliable employees and to conduct a complete investigation when a loss does occur. Complete information should be recorded so that facts can be compared whenever a loss occurs. A pattern may develop that thefts from guest rooms always seem to occur when a certain maid or houseman is assigned to that floor.

It is possible to exchange cylinders in locks to offset lost or stolen keys. Where a master key or a sub-master has been lost, however, the problem usually cannot be solved in this manner without tremendous expense.

In a smaller establishment such as a motel, lost or stolen room keys are usually not as severe a problem, since fewer locks are involved. Cylinders can be changed more easily without having to re-key the entire system.

Recently a new type of cylinder has been introduced which facilitates economic re-keying of hotel rooms. The cylinder fits into existing jamb hardware just as conventional cylinders do, and is compatible with several standard brands of lock. Installation requires no carpentry or wiring. Once inserted, the cylinder can be re-keyed in minutes. It does not require change of any of the keys up and down the line interrelated mathematically to master and grandmaster. The lock is also highly resistant to picking. A system of this type can reduce the costs of re-keying substantially.

The cylinder also has a second keyslot which is operative only by maids or other service personnel. This second slot operates the door lock only when the deadbolt is open, thereby eliminating disturbance of guests. This lock, like the guest's, can be re-keyed without requiring systemwide changeover.

Selecting Door Hardware

Whatever type of lock is used, it should be of sufficient quality to preclude the use of a celluloid strip or simple skeleton key to open the door. The most expensive lock is not necessarily the best, but the less expensive will most likely not provide the security desired. A competent locksmith can be of great assistance in choosing a lock.

An additional matter must be considered when selecting hardware for doors. We not only want to prevent illegal entry into a guest room in the absence of the guest, but we also want to give him protection and privacy while he is in the room. Every bedroom door should lock automatically when closed. Where it is required to put a key in the lock in order to activate the locked position, guests going out quite often forget and leave their doors unlocked. Locking the door from the inside with the use of a key is acceptable, and most hotel bedroom locks operate in this manner. When this is done, a signal device on the outside indicates the room is occupied and prevents maids from attempting to enter. In addition, it is well to provide the guest with an additional measure of security such as a chain or a dead latch.

Any number of devices can be installed to ensure complete security and prevent anyone from entering the room short of breaking down the entire door. Unfortunately, these extremes are impractical, as the innkeeper must be able to enter the room in the event of an emergency. People may become ill, commit suicide, die of natural causes, or become incapacitated and unable to open the door to admit help. Therefore, the locking devices used should give a degree of protection to the guest but, at the same time, be accessible to management.

With the increase in the number of guest room robberies committed in the presence of the guest, it would be well to consider the use of one-way "peepholes" in bedroom doors so that the guest can see who is knocking at the door without having to open it.

Where sliding glass doors are installed, they should have locking devices on the inside only. An additional security device can be provided by way of a metal bar which lies in the track of the door and prevents it from being opened.

Where French doors are used on outside balconies, the glass in them should be something other than normal window glass which can be easily broken, permitting the thief to reach in and unlock any device on the interior. Most areas have Fire Codes or Life Safety Codes outlawing the use of transoms; however, some older buildings may still have transoms. These present a security hazard since a small, thin person can sometimes slip through them.

In addition, they are very dangerous from a fire protection standpoint. A louvered door is also vulnerable to intrusion. Normally the louver frame can be knocked out easily, permitting admittance.

Keyless Locking Systems

For years, the test of negligence relative to theft from a guest room was whether or not there was forced entry to the room. Unless the plaintiff could show that his room was broken into, in most cases the innkeeper would not be held liable. This is no longer the case, as the courts have held that where the lock protecting the door is inadequate and easily compromised or circumvented, the innkeeper can be held liable. A guest has the right to assume that the lock on his room door will make him and his belongings secure. If it can be shown that the lock does not provide this security, the innkeeper can be found liable.

With such a trend developing, a new concept in locking devices is welcomed by security-minded owners. A number of successful new systems have been developed which eliminate the old traditional metal key with the associated costs of providing key blanks and cutting replacement keys, the need to replace lock cylinders, and other means currently undertaken to protect guests. These new computer-controlled systems utilizing a plastic "key" provide an unlimited range of security features that include more than guest room protection. The system can be integrated with the entire lock and key control system throughout the building; it can be used to facilitate guest charges in restaurants, bars and other satellite operations; it can control entry to restricted areas, as well as a number of other services.

The tremendous benefit realized by these keyless systems is that a single lock—or every lock—can be reprogrammed in a matter of minutes at a reasonable cost (pennies) as compared to the cost of several dollars to provide a new key blank and to "cut" a new key, or thirty to forty dollars to provide a new secure cylinder. Without a doubt, the new "card" system is the "key" of tomorrow. The only problem is the relatively high cost; however, recent improvements in the system have reduced the cost and have made this system far more attractive and within the financial reach of the smaller operator.

Windows

Entry to a room can be made through a window as well as a door. If a room happens to be on the 19th floor and there is no outside ledge, the opportunity of gaining admittance in this manner is greatly reduced. In many cases where air conditioning has been installed, the windows are sealed and admittance cannot be gained short of breaking the window. Even where air conditioning does exist, quite often one window is left unlocked or unsealed so that the occupant can obtain fresh air if he desires. In such cases, some type of device must be provided so the window can be locked. A catch installed in the center of a double-hung window provides very little protection, as only a small break in the glass is necessary to allow the thief to reach in, unfasten the catch and lift the window.

There are any number of devices that offer considerable window protection. It must be remembered that it is not necessary to make the device one that management can circumvent, as is the case with the door. A window device can and should be absolutely secure short of breaking the window itself to gain entry.

Windows present a particular hazard where air conditioning does not exist and the window is the only form of ventilation. This is true quite often in some older buildings. To make matters worse, these windows may open onto a common balcony accessible to anyone. There is no real answer to this problem. Heavy metal screens, windows that will lock in a given position not large enough to allow entry, bars on the windows, are all possibilities but are objectionable to many people. It is felt that the only answer from management's standpoint is to provide an acceptable lock for the window; if the guest decides not to keep the window locked, that becomes his risk.

In a motel, especially if units are arranged at ground level, illegal breaking and entering present a special problem. Attractive, heavy window screens can be employed, or windows can be alarmed to prevent illegal entry through breaking. Proper lighting along exterior walls and the absence of shrubs and other cover material will reduce the natural cover for the window thief. Occasional patrols around the property by the proprietor at unannounced times may indicate attempted entries or problem areas, and may deter the potential thief from an attempt.

EMPLOYEES ENTERING GUEST ROOMS

Certain employees must enter guest rooms for the purpose of cleaning, repairs, etc. It is hoped that these employees will all be honest and trustworthy. Unfortunately, such is not always the case. No one has a better opportunity to steal from a guest room than those with a legitimate reason to be in the room. When a group of employees band together in a conspiracy, the problem is intensified. For example, suppose a maid steals some valuables from a guest's room while in the process of cleaning. She hides the stolen merchandise on her person, on her maid's cart or in her supply closet. A houseman delivering clean linen to the maid picks up the stolen merchandise and hides it in his locker or perhaps passes it on to a yardman. The yardman, having access to the outside of the building, passes it along to a confederate on the street. The theft is completed, and it is going to be a difficult case to solve. As mentioned before, complete reports should be kept of such cases to see if a pattern develops.

Inspections Required

Supply closets and maid's carts are the property of the hotel and can be inspected by supervisory personnel at any time. Inspectresses and security officers should make routine checks regularly. At best, these inspections may be a deterrent; at least the employees will know that someone is watching them. Some employees may object, stating that they are under suspicion and are being treated as common criminals. It can be pointed out to these employees that the inspection is for their own good, as a third party may have hidden stolen goods in their equipment or storage rooms. If and when a loss is reported by a guest, an immediate search should be made of all possible hiding places in the vicinity.

It should be the policy of the hotel that every guest room must be inspected at least once every 24 hours regardless of whether the room is occupied. There are a number of reasons for the policy.

1. Mechanical breakdowns may occur that should be discovered as soon as possible, such as a lavatory that will not stop running or a leak in a pipe.

2. Lights or television sets may be left on inadvertently.
3. The room may have been disturbed in some way and be in no condition to receive a guest.
4. Where a "Do Not Disturb" sign remains on a room door over 24 hours and no activity has been seen or heard in the room, management should be notified and the matter investigated. Deaths often occur under such circumstances, and it is most desirable that such incidents be discovered as soon as possible.
5. "Skippers" or thefts of hotel property from rooms can be discovered.

Room Count

Normally, a room count is made by the maid as soon as she comes on duty. Where there is some indication that a guest is in the room—the "Do Not Disturb" sign is on the door or the indicator button on the lock shows the room is occupied—the maid merely reports the room occupied. Where there is no such indication, the maid enters the room. If it is vacant, she indicates this on her report. These reports are forwarded to the office, where they are checked against the hotel register. Any discrepancies should be investigated at once. This investigation is usually handled by the housekeeping department and constitutes merely a recheck of conditions. If a real discrepancy does occur, the security officer can immediately look into the matter.

Maid's Observations Valuable

In the process of a maid's work in a guest room, a great deal of information can be gathered which might be of considerable help to the security department. Anything of an unusual nature should be reported by the maid to her supervisor or to the security department. Such observation might include:

1. The presence of luggage without the normal contents, such as clothing. Many persons intent upon stealing property from a hotel room will fill their luggage with bricks, old telephone books or other useless material, dispose of these items and pack their bags with the hotel's linens, blankets, television parts, etc. If a maid spots such empty suitcases, her report of the incident can put the security department on the alert.

2. Firearms or weapons of any type seen in the guest room. They may be legitimate; however, it is better to have the matter investigated by the security department.

3. Evidence of any illegal activity. Gambling equipment, drug paraphernalia, etc., should be reported.

4. Any evidence of damage to the room, such as broken furniture or equipment, a fire, or evidence that someone has suffered physical harm, such as blood spattered on the walls.

5. Evidence that hotel property has been removed and that the guest is no longer an occupant of the room.

6. Any condition in the room that might be harmful to the guest. Guest safety considerations are discussed in detail in Chapter 6.

THEFT DETERRENT MEASURES

Removal of property by a guest is especially easy in motels, where the guest often parks his car adjacent to his room and can go from room to car without passing through a lobby or other supervised area. It may also occur in hotels where the guest may use a fire tower stairway to depart from the hotel. If a parking lot is nearby, stolen property can be transferred to a waiting vehicle quickly and easily by this means. (More will be said on the problem of fire towers in Chapter 7.)

Anti-Theft Equipment

There are several suggestions to deter theft of articles from guest rooms. Articles can be fastened securely to walls or tables with tamperproof hardware. While this will not be a failsafe method, it may prevent some people from stealing the items. Providing plastic bags to guests for packing shoes or wet bathing suits might prevent theft of towels, since this is the purpose for which towels are often taken. Towels and other items are also sometimes taken as souvenirs. An inexpensive item offered for sale might reduce such thefts. For example, one hotel offered an inexpensive towel with the inscription "Stolen from XYZ Hotel" and found it to be a popular item.

In some hotels, alarm systems have been installed which signal when an appliance has been removed from its normal location or position. If possible, such a system should be planned during the construction stage of a hotel or motel; however, it can be added later if desired. There are also "bugging" systems whereby an item is provided with a small sensor with a detector in the door jamb. If an article is carried through the doorway, the sensor activates the detector, which in turn sounds an alarm in the front office.

ID Markings

The use of a program similar to the "Operation Identification" program for homeowners can be instituted in a hotel or motel. Under this system, items are marked by an engraving tool with an inconspicuous identifying number or mark. In the event the item is stolen and later recovered, the real owner can be immediately identified. Hotels should record serial numbers of equipment and, if possible, items should carry some distinctive mark that can be identified at a later time. Such identifying marks are also important since some guests bring personal belongings into their rooms. Many people, for example, carry their own pillows due to allergies. A person leaving the hotel with a pillow under his arm might look suspicious . . . but unless the hotel can prove the pillow is the property of the hotel, a problem might develop.

Any guest who is observed leaving the hotel in an abnormal manner, such as down a fire escape, should be detained until his room can be inspected and it is determined that his account with the hotel has been settled.

Thefts should be reported to the police immediately. This requires that license numbers be recorded of all vehicles belonging to guests. The guest may have registered under a false name, but the license number can be traced by police to ascertain true identity. Stolen items found in the vehicle which can be identified through ID markings will be returned; the thief can be apprehended.

INVESTIGATING CLAIMS OF LOSS
FROM ROOMS

When a loss is reported, it should be investigated by the security officer immediately. The claimant should be interviewed personally by the security officer and the following information obtained:

1. Full name and address of the claimant.
2. Description of the missing items (as complete as possible).
3. When was the item last seen by the claimant and when was the loss discovered?
4. Did the claimant have any visitors in the room? Is the claimant suspicious of anyone in particular? If so, what occurred to make the claimant suspicious?
5. What is the value of the missing item(s) and were they insured? If so, by whom?

If at all possible, this information should be taken in writing, either recorded by the investigator or written out by the claimant. After as much information as possible has been recorded, the statement should be signed by the claimant. If the claimant refuses to make a written statement or to sign the statement, this fact should be noted.

Inspection of Room

Following this, the investigating officer should indicate that he desires to examine the guest's room. The claimant should be requested to remain in the security office or the lobby and should not accompany the investigator. The investigation of the room should include, but not be limited to, the following:

1. Is there any sign of forced entry into the room?
2. Are all locks and locking devices in proper working condition?
3. A search should be made of the room for the missing items. Care must be taken not to disturb the property of the guest; however, a very thorough search should be made.
4. The floor maid should be interviewed to determine whether she has any information about the loss. Did the maid ever see the missing item in the guest's room? Did she witness anyone entering or leaving the room? Did the guest make any comments regarding the loss?

Many Losses Accidental

Quite often a reported theft turns out to be an accidental loss and the item is located in the room. A lady may remove her jewelry, wrap it in a tissue and hide it under the mattress, pin it to the pillow, or hide it in some other place. Unfortunately, the next morning she may forget what she did the night before; missing the item, she immediately claims a robbery.

When such a loss is reported, beds should be completely stripped and the linen carefully examined. Mattresses should be raised as well as cushions. Every possible hiding place should be examined and every place where the item may have fallen should be checked. If the wastebasket has not been emptied, the contents should be carefully examined. A ring wrapped in a tissue might appear to be a used tissue and be thrown away by the owner.

Search in Other Areas

If the lost item is not located in the guest room, additional areas may be searched, depending on what the missing item is. A missing purse or wallet, for example, will often be found in a stairway, behind a radiator, in a trash container or in some other location where a thief thas thrown it after removing the money or valuables. Naturally the thief does not want to take a chance on being apprehended with the wallet in his possession. The fact that he has money in his pocket when apprehended is not in itself absolutely incriminating.

If the stolen article is clothing or jewelry, it is probably hidden someplace on the property or has already been removed from the premises. Storage rooms, maid's carts, lockers and other hiding places should be carefully checked. If there is any suspicion of fraud on the part of the guest (that the item has been thrown away deliberately in order to collect insurance, for example), trash chutes should be examined as well as other hiding places.

Reporting the Loss

In the event that a loss of jewelry or other valuables appears legitimate, the police should be notified so that pawnbrokers can be alerted. The claimant should be advised to report the loss to his own insurance company. At no time in the investigation should the security officer or any member of management make any statement as to liability in the case. No admissions should be made and no denials offered, but rather every possible fact should be gathered, recorded and forwarded to the hotel's insurance agent for action. The responsibility for reporting the loss to the local police rests with the guest; however, the security officer may assist the guest in contacting the police as a courtesy.

The importance of the initial interview with the guest cannot be overstated. Quite often the true story emerges as the facts in the matter are probed. A striking example of this occurs frequently when a man reports a sum of money stolen from his trousers or wallet. Under questioning it will be determined that he had been out on the town in the company of a young lady the previous night. The possibility that he was "rolled" has entered his mind, but he does not wish to be embarrassed by this loss. If he can blame it on the hotel, his conscience will be cleared and he can get his money back. Any time a claimant appears to be "hung over" when making a loss claim, the security officer should be suspicious and investigate carefully the events that occurred prior to the loss.

SUMMARY

The hotel is obligated to provide a reasonable degree of protection for the guest and his property while in the room assigned to him. Naturally, the hotel does not wish any guest to suffer a loss; however, once the hotel provides the accepted physical and mechanical protection devices, institutes rules and regulations designed to protect the guest and makes the guest aware of what protection is available, the hotel cannot be held liable for a loss if the guest fails to avail himself of the protection offered.

Unfortunately, some guests are quick to blame the innkeeper when something goes wrong regardless of how careless they have been themselves. A classic example occurs frequently in some older hotels not equipped with air conditioning. On a warm evening a guest may open his window and then prop his door open in order to get cross-ventilation. While he is asleep, there is nothing to stop anyone from entering the room, removing valuables lying on the bureau and departing completely undetected. Who will be blamed for the loss? The innkeeper. Even though the claim would never be allowed in a court of law, the guest will still blame the innkeeper and may tell his friends how he was "robbed blind" while at the XYZ Hotel.

Chapter 6

Responsibility for the Guest's Safety

The definition of security includes safety—freedom from danger or hazard. Security considerations for public areas in the hotel, such as hallways, lobbies, and specific public rooms, must include safety—the safety of the guest, patron, visitor, or employee (although responsibility for employee safety is governed by a different set of rules; see Chapter 7). Responsibility for safety in these cases rests not only on the innkeeper, but also on the other party. As far as the innkeeper is concerned, his responsibility cannot be transferred to a third party. Perhaps a few examples of cases that have been adjudicated will be helpful in understanding the problem.

COURT DECISION ON LIABILITY

A number of years ago, there was a famous case concerning a hotel guest who left his room carrying a number of articles and became confused in his directions. Instead of going to the regular guest elevators, he arrived at a freight elevator. The door to this elevator was open although the cab itself was on a lower level. The guest stepped into the opening and fell into the elevator shaft, suffering serious injuries.

Guest Need Not Look for Danger

A number of legal premises arose from this case which have been applied to similar incidents. First, the court has declared that a guest of a hotel need not look for dangers. He has the right to presume that the innkeeper has exercised care and has provided a safe premises. However, the concept has been added that the guest must exercise reasonable diligence and reasonable care such as ordinary prudent persons would exercise under like circumstances.

For example, if the innkeeper left the door to an elevator open and provided no warning or safety device to prevent an accident, the innkeeper would be liable for injuries due to this lack of care for the guest's safety. This would be true even if the elevator was in the control of a third party, such as a contractor engaged in making repairs. However, the guest could not recover damages, in spite of the innkeeper's neglect of duty, if he himself was negligent. If the guest was familiar with the elevator, found the door partially open, pushed it further open and fell in, his recovery would be barred by contributory negligence.

Proving Negligence

In cases where the plaintiff charges negligence on the part of the innkeeper, usually it will be necessary for the plaintiff to show by competent evidence the following factors:

1. That a dangerous situation was present;
2. That such dangerous situation remained long enough to give the defendant reasonable notice of its existence;
3. That the defendant, after having such notice, nevertheless failed to remove the danger or warn the plaintiff of its existence;
4. That as a result of this condition the plaintiff was injured;
5. That damages should be awarded commensurate with the injuries.

CLEANING HAZARDS

Wet Floors

Lobby areas and stairways are usually cleaned during the night hours. Marble or tile areas are usually cleaned with some form of liquid with a soap or detergent. Wet marble can be very slippery and dangerous unless a person walks carefully. If under such conditions the innkeeper were to place a warning sign at the beginning of the work area, and/or to block the area in some manner, in most cases this would be accepted as sufficient notice that a dangerous condition existed and that persons in the area should take reasonable care. If a guest were to run through the cleaning area or proceed in some other unsafe manner, and sustained an injury due to a fall, in all probability this would be considered contributory negligence on the guest's part.

Vacuum Cords

A hazard may exist also where hallways are being cleaned with a vacuum cleaner. A guest may trip over the cord stretched down the hallway and fall. The safest manner of handling this situation is to place a sign in the hallway at the start of the work area, advising the guest to watch his step. In addition, if the cleaner confines his work to one side or one half of the area, keeping the cord in a straight line behind him, the guest can walk on the opposite side of the work area.

HAZARDS IN GUEST ROOMS

Safety hazards that may occur in guest rooms include a frayed or excessively long extension cord that a guest could trip over; a worn spot in a carpet that could cause a guest to trip; a broken, chipped or damaged piece of furniture that could cause a cut or other damage to a guest; cracked or damaged plaster that could fall and cause injury; loose handrails in showers or bathtubs; damaged toilet seats; chipped drinking glasses, etc.

Negligence Doctrine

Any hazard in the room causing injury to a guest could be the basis of a negligence suit by the injured party. In such a legal action for negligence, the doctrine of *res ipsa loquitur* is a rule of evidence often applied. Translated as "The thing speaks for itself," the doctrine is usually applied where:

1. The thing or instrumentality causing the injury is under

the exclusive control of the defendant or his employees at the time of the injury;

2. The accident is such as does not happen in the ordinary course if those who have jurisdiction and responsibility use proper care.

Where the doctrine is applied, the defendant has the burden of explaining his failure or inability to control the situation.

Injury Claims

As indicated earlier, the fact that an area or piece of equipment is in the control of a third party does not relieve the innkeeper of his liability in case of injury to a guest. Wherever a dangerous or potentially dangerous condition exists, the innkeeper should take every precaution to isolate the danger by the use of signs, barricades, gates, doors or whatever is necessary.

The potential for injury claims is almost limitless. Every time a guest sustains an injury of any kind in a hotel, his first impulse seems to be to blame the innkeeper, regardless of how much he may have contributed to the accident himself. For this reason it is well to be certain that every accident is investigated fully and carefully and that the hotel carries sufficient liability insurance. Actual lawsuits against hotels have involved accidents such as: stubbing a toe on the foot of a bed; tripping over rugs or pieces of furniture; being scalded in a shower or bathtub; slipping and falling on floors, shower stalls, bathtubs, dance floors; collapse of chairs; splinters from chairs and beds; injuries from articles that have fallen or been pushed over accidentally; cuts from chipped glasses, mirrors or table tops; pinched fingers from doors, drawers or windows; as well as many claims of being served unfit food or beverage (see Chapter 9).

We can only repeat that if the innkeeper is aware of any condition where an injury may result, or if he should be aware of the situation under normal conditions, he is obligated to take such action as is necessary to correct the situation. The innkeeper is not an insurer of the safety of his guests, but he does have a duty to exercise reasonable care for the guest's safety and comfort. As long as he discharges this duty, the innkeeper cannot be held liable if a guest is injured through his own negligence.

DANGER OF FALLING ITEMS

A serious hazard in hotels concerns persons walking outside who are struck by items falling or thrown from the hotel. There are many cases where a portion of a building itself has fallen, injuring a passer-by. A piece of cornice, a brick, piece of slate, window screen, or some other part of the building can become dislodged and fall to the street, with deadly results.

Possibility of Negligence

While each case must be considered in view of the facts surrounding the specific incident, the hotel is usually considered negligent. The physical condition of the building must be of prime concern to the innkeeper. Normally, bricks and other building parts do not become loose suddenly, but as a result of prolonged wear. Routine inspections are required to discover such conditions so that appropriate repairs can be made before the situation becomes serious. On the other hand, if lightning should strike a brick chimney, shattering the bricks and causing them to fall, the innkeeper would defend himself by denying he had any control over the situation. It was caused by a force outside his control, and he could not be held liable under the conditions.

Items Intentionally Thrown

Persons may also be injured by items falling or being thrown from the window of a room occupied by a guest. Youngsters, as well as some adults acting like youngsters, enjoy throwing water bombs, firecrackers, cherry bombs, beer cans, bottles, ice and other assorted missiles from their windows. In all probability they do not intend to cause injury, but the results can be deadly. The innkeeper will be the first to be blamed.

Some of the factors we have previously discussed apply to such situations. The innkeeper under normal circumstances has no knowledge of what is occurring in a guest's room. The guest has control of that room for his own purpose and the innkeeper can only enter for good reason and just cause. Until a situation is brought to the innkeeper's attention, he has no way of knowing the danger; up to that point, he cannot be held responsible or liable. Once the innkeeper becomes aware of the impending or actual danger, he then must use his power to control the situation or be held in contributory negligence. If an innkeeper (or his agent or employee) is notified that items are being thrown from a window, he must make every attempt to identify the window from which the articles are being thrown and take the necessary steps to stop this activity.

Items Falling Accidentally

The situation may occur where a falling article was not intentionally thrown. It may have been placed on the window sill and accidentally knocked over, causing it to fall from the window. Again, the innkeeper cannot be held liable unless he was aware that such articles were on the window sill and posed a potential danger. The innkeeper is not required to inspect for such articles, since they do not come under the class of objects requiring inspection for proper maintenance. If a window screen should fall from a window or be pushed out accidentally, the innkeeper may be held liable; this would be an item subject to inspection and one which should be maintained in such a manner as to prevent an accident.

INJURY BY OTHER PERSONS

The innkeeper's duty to provide for the safety and comfort of the guest applies not only to the physical condition of the building but also to the conduct of guests and employees in relation to other guests as well as to themselves. Again, the innkeeper must be aware of dangerous situations and must do everything within his power to correct them or be held liable to contributory negligence.

Protection from Dangerous Persons

A case a number of years ago involved an intoxicated man who entered a female guest's room. The woman called the desk clerk and requested that the man be ejected from her room. This was done. Later she telephoned the desk clerk again and requested that the man be kept away from her room. A short time later, the woman was attacked by the same man in the hallway, badly beaten and injured. She brought suit against the hotel and the judge found in her favor. The basis for the finding was the fact that the hotel had been warned specifically that such an incident might occur; the lady had requested protection from the hotel. The hotel was aware of a dangerous or potentially dangerous situation, yet did not take any steps within its power to control it.

Incautious Actions

Several years ago a security officer observed a man sitting on a ledge outside his hotel window some nine stories above the ground. There was a parade in progress below, and it was obvious that the guest had taken this seat to obtain a better view. He was immediately contacted and ordered to reenter his room. The man was completely sober, apparently of sound mind, and had gone out on the ledge of his own free will and did not consider himself in any danger. Once this man was observed in that position, the hotel security officer was aware of a potential danger. Had the man fallen later without an attempt by the security officer to remove him from the ledge, the hotel could have been liable. If this situation were brought to the officer's attention and he replied, "If he's crazy enough to sit out there, that's his problem; if he falls, that's his tough luck," then the hotel would be guilty of negligence in not doing what it could to correct the situation.

"Horseplay" and Pranks

Many injuries occur due to "horseplay," not only between children but adults as well. Children running through hallways may knock down an elderly person. Convention delegates may remove fire hoses from wall stations and shoot water into a fellow delegate's room. In such a case, they are not only creating a potentially dangerous situation for the victim, but they are violating fire prevention codes in most localities by the misuse of emergency equipment.

If the innkeeper, his agents or employees witness or are made aware of such a dangerous situation, they must take the necessary steps to correct it. If two men are sitting at a bar and quite suddenly become involved in a fight, injuring a third party as a result, the hotel may be held liable if it can be shown that the bartender could see tempers rising and did nothing to prevent the fight in the first place. If there was no warning of the impending fight, then the bartender must take immediate steps to end it once it begins, before anyone, the combatants or third parties, are injured. Failure to do so would be viewed as negligence on the part of the barkeeper, who is an employee of the innkeeper, thereby making the innkeeper liable.

INJURY BY EMPLOYEES

The situation of an employee injuring a guest presents a problem. Different states have different interpretations of when the innkeeper may be held liable.

Innkeeper's Liability

In what is considered the Minority Rule in the United States, an injury sustained by a guest at the hands of an employee constitutes a breach of contract and the employer is held liable for the acts of his employees, whether such act is committed in the line of duty or not. The Majority Rule in the United States considers the injury as liability negligence and holds the innkeeper liable only when the employee is acting within the scope of his duties.

To state this another way, the innkeeper is not responsible for the torts of his employees unless those torts were committed in the conduct of business. The Minority Rule says in effect that the innkeeper has an obligation to see that his guests are not injured by the wrongful or negligent acts of his employees, regardless of whether they are acting within the scope of their employment. They are still employees, they are still on the premises, and therefore they should be under the control of the innkeeper. While the question may be academic in nature and will not become an issue until presented in court, the security officer should be aware of what doctrine applies within his locality. This knowledge may be important in gathering information and evidence when investigating a claim of injury.

Employees under the influence of alcohol or drugs should not be permitted on the premises. If an employee injured a guest in some way and was found to be under the influence of liquor, the hotel would be placed in a very bad position.

Contributory Negligence Factors

Injury to a guest need not be intentional but may well be accidental. In such a situation there may be contributory negligence on the part of the guest or a third party that would prevent recovery of damages by the injured party. Consider a situation where a waiter is pouring hot coffee into a patron's cup. As his attention is diverted for moment, he accidentally pours the coffee on the table and it splashes on the guest. The guest receives burns from the hot liquid and damage to clothing and brings a claim for personal injuries and property damage. If the facts in the case were just as outlined, in all probability the court would rule that the waiter was not exhibiting the attention he should have and the hotel would be held liable.

The situation would be different, however, if the incident occurred as follows. Just as the waiter was about to pour the coffee, he advised the guest of his intentions and the guest moved slightly to allow the waiter sufficient room to pour. Involved in conversation with a fellow diner, the guest made a sweeping gesture with his hand, striking the coffee pot and causing coffee to spill all over himself. In such a case, the waiter could not be held at fault and it would probably be considered contributory negligence on the part of the guest.

The same situation could occur if a third party happened to pass by and bump the waiter just as he was pouring the coffee. In this case an additional question might arise as to crowding in the dining room and whether this created an unsafe condition that was within the power of the innkeeper to control. If it was found that the third party was not watching where he was walking when he came into contact with the waiter, the verdict probably would be in favor of the innkeeper. If it was found that the dining room was so crowded that it was impossible to walk without brushing against tables, chairs, waiters or guests, the innkeeper might find himself accused of operating a dangerous situation.

INNKEEPER'S RESPONSIBILITY INCREASES

The court's application of the yardstick mentioned previously for determining negligence has changed recently, placing a far greater burden on the innkeeper. The concept of law that the innkeeper must provide reasonable security for his guests has also taken on a new meaning. What was reasonable years ago is not considered reasonable today. For example, the crime rate in all urban areas has increased greatly in the last decade and continues to grow. Hotels that were once located in quiet residential or business areas, where crimes of violence never took place, may find themselves located in the center of a crime-infested area because of changing economic conditions, increased population or other reasons. Crime has spread to every corner of our nation and every street in our cities. The criminals and the crimes they commit are not restricted to the streets and alleys, but now enter our public buildings, hotels and even homes. Muggings, rape, murder, arson, all take place daily, in broad daylight as well as under cover of darkness, and all citizens must be on the alert for such events.

Crime Record of the Hotel

The innkeeper must be aware of crime conditions. If he is to provide "reasonable care" for his guests, he must take steps to prevent criminal acts from occurring within his property. The "track record" of a hotel will be a powerful piece of evidence in the hands of the plaintiff in the event of a claim for injuries sustained at the hands of a third party within the hotel. How many incidents have occurred within the hotel or on its property? A record of various crimes is certainly reasonable notice to the hotel that a dangerous condition exists and that the existing security system is not capable of controlling the situation.

When management is confronted with arguments for increased security, the response often is: "What do you want to do, turn this hotel into an armed camp?" or "I can't vouch for those who enter my premises. How do I know what they are going to do after they rent a room from me or enter my building?"

It is not necessary to turn a hotel into an armed camp. It *is* necessary to take steps to provide as much security as would be considered reasonable and normal under the circumstances of the day. Watching the front door of the hotel while allowing the rear door to be open and unattended would not be considered good security. Access control is vital; if it is not administered, even the slightest degree of security cannot be established.

"Reasonable" Depends on Circumstances

Certainly, not all crime and all danger can be eliminated. Each incident must be judged on its own merits, and the actions taken by management will determine whether or not they would be considered reasonable. For example, if a man checked into a hotel, acted in a normal manner, was acceptably dressed, and after being roomed he removed a weapon from his suitcase and started a killing spree, management would have had no previous notice of a dangerous situation. They could not be held liable for allowing this person to enter the premises. Management's actions following the initial notification that there was an armed man on the premises would then have to be considered.

However, if a man came running into a hotel lobby carrying a weapon in plain sight and was allowed to ascend to the upper floors, there would be reason to question the actions of management in not detaining him at the entrance.

Another concept raised by innkeepers is the theory that "We aren't doing anything that every other hotel in town isn't doing. None of us have security officers *per se*. Security is handled by the assistant manager on duty. We have watchmen at night as required by law, and if there is any trouble during the day, we call the police. We all do this, so why charge that our hotel doesn't provide reasonable security?" The answer to such a statement can only be: What is customarily done in a given industry or trade is not the test of whether that conduct is reasonable. If that conduct is unreasonable for one hotel, it does not become reasonable just because every other hotel is also guilty of the same conduct.

ILLNESS OF A GUEST

Occasionally a guest or customer becomes ill while on the premises of a hotel or motel. What obligations does the innkeeper have to such a person? Does he have a duty to provide care or first aid? Generally the so-called Good Samaritan rule applies: the innkeeper has no legal obligation to help, but if help is volunteered, it must be given with reasonable care.

Legal Opinion

In a recent court case involving a claim against a hotel for failure to provide aid to an injured guest, the court stated, "The operator of a hotel owes no duty to perform any service for a guest who may become ill or injured. If, however, it undertakes to provide such service for any person, it must exercise care to provide such services as it has undertaken to give." What the court is saying is that if the hotel does agree to assist, that assistance must be qualified—that is, the services of a physician or at least a licensed professional nurse should be provided.

A distinction should be made between a situation in which the customer or guest becomes ill or suffers an accident without any negligence by the proprietor, and a situation in which an accident occurs that may have resulted from the proprietor's negligence. From a practical standpoint, the proprietor who anticipates an allegation of negligence may find it wise to make every effort to provide the best possible assistance.

Providing Emergency Care

An innkeeper must decide whether he should provide for emergency care on his premises. Many hotels have a registered nurse in attendance and many have a "house doctor" on call. If such facilities are not available, the innkeeper must decide in advance what is to be done when sickness or accidents are reported to him. A plan should be established and instructions given to all employees so that assistance can be provided without involving the hotel in a lawsuit.

The safest procedure for a hotel may be to notify the local emergency medical service and then merely to protect the sick or injured party from any additional danger. The important point to remember is that the establishment must do with care whatever it undertakes to do. Anyone sent to aid the ill person must be qualified. Under no circumstances should any drug or medicine be given to a sick or injured person unless administered by a qualified medical person. This is true even of such a common drug as aspirin.

When a person becomes sick or unconscious, hotel staff are advised to check for a "Medic Alert" bracelet or other vital information which may be worn or carried by persons with medical problems such as heart trouble, epilepsy, diabetes, etc. If such information is found, the attention of a doctor or nurse should be drawn to it, since special action or medication may be urgently needed.

The care of sick or injured persons becomes a matter of public relations. To turn one's back on the sick and injured is not in keeping with the ideal of helping one's brother or of doing unto others as you would have them do unto you. However, there is an important difference between attempting to secure *qualified* assistance and attempting to solve the problem oneself. A little knowledge can be a dangerous thing, especially when one is dealing with the life and health of an injured party. Certain emergencies require immediate action, but *improper* action can cause more serious problems. The best advice for the innkeeper is, "Get qualified help, and know in advance where to get that help."

SUMMARY

The entire subject of the safety of guests and patrons in public places deals with people. It is difficult at best to determine what people are going to do. The law does not expect an innkeeper to be clairvoyant, but only to use reasonable good sense, provide reasonable care to ensure the safety of his guests and to take the necessary action to remove or relieve dangerous situations when they are brought to his attention.

The question whether reasonable care was taken will be one for a jury to decide. Juries are people, and, again, people are unpredictable. The security officer must be aware of potential hazards, must search for hazards and take steps to remove or control them in the name of the innkeeper.

The hotel is concerned with the safety of the guest, whether he is in his assigned room or in the public areas of the hotel. In addition, the hotel invites the public to use a portion of its facilities. While the hotel's responsibility to the guest and to the invited patron may differ in degree, the innkeeper wants to avoid any injuries or unpleasantness as far as possible. Where the statutes or other legal requirements have been established to control its operation, the hotel wants to be sure to abide by these regulations. Safety and security go hand in hand, and the security officer must always bear this in mind.

Chapter 7

Controlling Access to Non-Public Areas

The terms "front of the house" and "back of the house" are common throughout the hotel industry. While some services obviously take place in both areas of the hotel, the actual physical separation between those areas designated for the use of the guest and those where the guest is not normally allowed distinguish the "front" from the "back" of the house.

"BACK OF THE HOUSE" SECURITY

It should be quite apparent why guests and visitors should not have free access to hotel service areas. Not only would the added traffic create confusion, but certain hazards may exist to which the innkeeper does not wish to expose guests. In addition, the hotel must protect itself against theft and other crimes. Security in the back of the house is just as important and can be far stricter than that exercised in the front of the house.

Know Who Enters and Why

At all times hotel security should know who is in the building and for what purpose they are there. Unless a person is known and has a reason for being in the hotel, he should not be permitted to enter. Security officers or other employees observing a suspicious person in hallways leading to bedrooms should confront the suspect to determine his business. If the suspect claims to be a guest, he should have a room key in his possession or be able to identify the room assigned to him. If he does not have a key but states he is in a particular room, his name should be asked. It is then a simple matter to call the hotel desk to determine if a guest by that name is indeed registered in that room. If there is any discrepancy, assistance should be requested at once and the subject kept under surveillance if possible.

If a suspicious person is observed in public areas, he too should be approached and asked to state his business. If he cannot give a good account of himself, he should be asked to leave the premises and should be escorted to the nearest exit.

Identifying Badges for Visitors

If strangers are observed in completely restricted areas, such as service areas where only employees should be, they should be stopped, questioned and escorted from the area. Under certain circumstances the innkeeper may wish to allow certain persons into restricted areas. Under such conditions, these persons should be provided with some identifying badge, button or mark recognizable by all employees. In this way they will not be stopped and questioned repeatedly by well-meaning, security-conscious employees or security personnel.

Designation of "Employees Only" Areas

There is no assumed invitation to enter the back of the house as there is the front. As we discussed earlier, a person may enter the public areas of a hotel under the assumption that he is invited, and the innkeeper may revoke that invitation if he desires. Before a person may enter the back of the house, however, he must *in fact* be invited to do so; if he enters without this permission, he is guilty of trespassing. For this reason, areas that are considered "off limits" or "restricted" must be clearly designated and some form of physical barrier, such as a door, should be provided.

Doors leading from public areas to service areas to permit passage of service employees should be kept closed at all times, not only to prevent the passage of unauthorized persons but also to maintain a fire stop. These doors serve a dual purpose, but in order to be effective they must be kept closed . . . not necessarily locked, but closed. On the face of the door in easily visible letters should appear the indication of the door's purpose. If it is for the passage of employees, the sign might read "Employees Only" or "Authorized Personnel Only." If the door leads to a planned recognized exit, the sign should so state. No one would consider establishing rest rooms without indicating "Women" or "Men" on the proper door, and the same consideration should be given to every other door available to the guests. If a person opens an unmarked door, enters in all innocence and is injured, the innkeeper may be held liable. However, if that same person enters a door which is properly marked indicating that entrance is limited to authorized persons only, and he is injured, the question of liability on the part of the innkeeper would be seriously questioned.

SUPERVISION OF ENTRANCES

In addition to entrances to service areas within the hotel itself, there are entrances from the outside—employee entrances, delivery entrances, service entrances. At times these may be kept locked; when they are open, they should be under the supervision of a guard or security personnel. Any person entering through a service entrance should be identified, his reason for entering known and verified, and any packages or other items he carries in should be inspected or checked with the guard. A permanent record should be made of every person entering or leaving.

A variety of persons will enter and depart through service areas, including employees, salesmen, service personnel, and deliverymen. A discussion of the methods of handling each is in order.

Most persons entering service areas will be employees. Some hotels allow white collar workers to enter through the front door of the hotel and require only service employees to enter through the employee entrance. This is a matter of policy that must be decided by management; however, we feel that better control can be maintained if all employees enter at the same location.

Employee ID

Some form of identification must be provided to all employees which should be kept upon their person at all times when they are on the premises. The form of identification will depend in great measure on the number of employees involved, the rate of turnover and the type of security at the entrance. Many employees are required to punch a time card upon entering and departing the building. If the cards are located at the entrance, the employee's time card serves as proof that he belongs in the hotel. If separate "In" and "Out" racks are maintained for the cards, anyone can tell at a glance which employees are in the hotel at any given time. However, time cards alone are not adequate to maintain good security when a large number of employees are involved. Anyone could walk in, take a time card, punch it in, and go about the hotel at will.

The same holds true where only a badge is used as identification, as a person intent on gaining entrance could steal a badge, or, if working in collusion with an employee, gain access to a badge which would give him free access to the hotel. An identification card with the holder's picture offers a far greater degree of security. Where the number of employees is small and each employee is known to the guard or to management, these security measures may not be necessary. If some form of identification is used, an absolute system must be devised to ensure the surrender of identification when an employee is discharged and to require that notice be given in the event an employee loses his identification. The whole object of having a guard or some type of security at the employee entrance is to ensure that anyone claiming to be an employee is, in fact, just that and is entitled to enter the premises.

Package Checks

Employees should not be permitted to enter the premises with personal belongings unless the contents are inspected and noted. Such items as shopping bags, luggage or boxes should be checked with the guard until the employee leaves, or should be opened and inspected. Such inspection is even more important upon the employee's departure.

An example will help point out the reason for this security measure. Mary Jones comes to work at 4:00 p.m. as a night maid. She enters the hotel service entrance carrying a large shopping bag. She is known to the guard on duty, who watches her punch her time card. In reply to his question she states that she has just done some shopping and did not have time to go home to leave her purchases. Without inspecting the shopping bag, the guard lets Mary enter the hotel. Going to her locker, she changes into her uniform and goes about her duties. At quitting time, Mary empties her shopping bag (which contained only paper and a few empty boxes), fills it with sheets and towels, places an empty wrapped box on top and leaves to "check out." Passing the guard again, she rings her time card out, says good-night and goes her way, four sheets and a dozen towels to the good.

Instituting a package check system could prevent this theft. Mary's shopping bag could be inspected when she entered the building, or she could be required to check it with the guard, a more acceptable system. Suppose, however, that Mary was very clever and, even though the bag was inspected, the packages were all gift-wrapped and had some weight to them. The guard would not require her to open each package and would allow her to enter the building with her bag. Upon departure, Mary would be required to produce a package pass from her immediate supervisor stating the contents of the bag and granting permission to leave the building with the bag. The guard would be required at this point to check the contents of the bag against the contents listed on the pass. No supervisor should issue a pass for any item until he has seen the contents. If Mary were forced to open each package regardless of the fact they were gift-wrapped, she would soon make other arrangements for her legitimate packages.

This security measure will meet with opposition when first placed in operation. It requires complete cooperation between supervisors and security personnel. However, once it is effectively instituted and conscientiously administered, there should be no further trouble from this particular problem.

Search Considerations

Another problem occurs, however, that is more difficult to cope with. This is the carrying on one's person of stolen items. As those in the retail business are concerned with shoplifters and pilferers and the many ways they have devised for removing articles from stores, so too is the innkeeper faced with the same problem. It is very easy to place some silverware in an overcoat pocket or in a pants pocket. It is very easy to wrap a table cloth or a sheet around the body under a shirt or dress. Any number of items can be transported on the human body. Even if only a few are taken at a time, over a period of a few weeks the losses can be great.

Aside from a personal search of the individual, either by hand or by mechanical devices, there is no proven way of overcoming such stealing. To subject each employee to such a search would surely result in suits charging violation of civil rights if not outright rebellion by the employees. Occasional spot checks, however, might be permitted. Certainly overcoats carried over the arm or with bulging pockets can be examined by an alert guard. In the case of a highly suspicious person, the cooperation of the local police may result in a stop-and-frisk upon departure from the hotel premises.

Advice should be secured from legal counsel as to the rights of search as they apply in a given location. To search an employee or his vehicle is, in most cases, illegal without lawful justification. The question immediately arises as to what is lawful justification, and it is this point that should be made clear by counsel. If, as part of the employment contract, the employee gives written consent to the search of his person or his automobile while on the hotel premises, the innkeeper then has the legal right to conduct such a search. In addition to a discussion with counsel, the appropriate labor unions representing the employees should be apprised of the policy to be followed and the methods to be employed.

Finally, if bodily searches are to be conducted, a female employee should be searched by a female security officer. No male officer should undertake the search of a female except in extreme circumstances where the question of a hidden weapon may be involved and there is a reasonable concern that this weapon may be used against the officer. Even in such cases it is wiser to have a female present as a witness.

Other Theft Preventive Measures

Obviously, the best preventive to employee stealing is to provide controls and restrictions that make it almost impossible to secure the desired merchandise in the first place. Remove the opportunity to steal, and the chances of loss are reduced.

Naturally, no system is foolproof, and many people spend their lives trying to beat the system. There will always be some stealing going on that security must guard against. If there are tight controls, the thief is forced to act on the spur of the moment. He cannot pick and choose the time he will steal his desired item; he must grab it when he can.

This means the thief must hide the article in some place until he is ready to remove it from the premises. One possible hiding place may be in his locker or in a closet or storage room under his direct control. These hiding places can be eliminated very easily. Part of the hiring procedure is to issue the new employee a locker and a key or lock for that locker. It is legal to have a statement on the locker assignment slip stating that the employee gives management the right to search his locker at any time, in the presence of the employee. The employee signs this assignment slip, acknowledging receipt of the locker and key and giving management this right. If at a later date the security officer feels stolen items are being hidden in the employee's locker, he has the right to have the locker opened and make an inspection.

The same right holds true where employees are permitted to park their cars on hotel property. Part of the contract for parking includes the right of management to search the car at its discretion while it is on hotel property. If the car is parked on public property, neither management nor the police have the right to search the car unless armed with a proper search warrant.

Closets, storerooms and the like are under the direct control of management and may be inspected at any time. A linen closet is for the storage of linen and a maid's closet is for the storage of her supplies and materials. Personal property should not be kept in such places, and supervisors should be firm in enforcing such regulations.

OTHERS USING SERVICE ENTRANCES

Salesmen

Another group entering the service entrances of a hotel will be salesmen. In some organizations, all purchasing is done through a central purchasing office, while in other cases individual department heads are permitted to do a limited amount of their own purchasing. In either case, salesmen will be outsiders coming into the hotel, supposedly on legitimate business, who will want access to offices or persons within the building.

All such persons should be stopped by security personnel at the entrance, asked to identify themselves, their business and whom they wish to see. A call should then be placed by the guard to the hotel employee involved, to determine whether the employee is available and if he desires to see this particular individual. To accommodate salesmen who call every day or on a very regular basis, the guard might be given a list of the names of those who are permitted to enter the building.

Once it has been determined that a person is entitled to enter, that person should be given a visitor's badge to be worn as long as he is in the building. In addition, the person's name should be entered in a log book together with the time of entry, destination, and time of departure. In this way a constant record is provided of everyone entering and leaving the building and the time each visitor spent in the building.

In the event the visitor does not know the location of the office he seeks, an escort should be provided for him. Employees should be aware of visitor's badges so that if they see a person wandering around wearing such a badge, they can offer assistance or escort the visitor to the proper location. Any stranger seen in the back of the house not having a visitor's badge should be escorted to the nearest security guard or the security office. This becomes a duty imposed on each employee, and it must be explained to them by management so they will know exactly what is expected of them and how they are to act.

Deliverymen

All types of materials and supplies will be delivered to the hotel. The hotel has the right to designate certain hours for deliveries and should do so in order to have a responsible person on hand to accept and handle deliveries. Normally, deliveries should be made to the loading platform of a hotel, from which point the hotel employees take over. There is no reason why deliverymen should enter the hotel premises. If, for any reason, it is necessary or desirable for the deliveryman to enter the hotel to place his deliveries any place but the loading dock, he should be accompanied by a responsible representative of management. Material received at the service entrance should be checked as to number of pieces, correct weight (if weight is a factor), condition of items and proper invoicing before the receiving clerk takes custody.

In the same respect, items will be removed from the premises through this service entrance. Display goods may be shipped by outside carrier and will be dispatched from the hotel through this exit. As with incoming goods, outgoing items should be covered with a proper bill of lading or some proof of what is going out with the proper authority for the dispatching. A written record should be kept of all items received or dispatched.

Trash Pick-Up

Trash and garbage may be removed from the hotel to an outside holding shed for pick-up by the appropriate contractors. These items will also leave the premises via the service area. Extreme vigilance is required when trash is removed, since this is a very popular method of removing stolen goods. A load of presumably empty cartons may contain supplies, foodstuffs or any type of merchandise stashed by a thief for later removal. Naturally, it is almost impossible for any guard to go through all the trash, and it would be unreasonable for him to sift through a load of garbage. Certain regulations can be instituted to lessen the chances of such deception, however.

The hotel may require that all cardboard cartons and tin cans be flattened. This will not only prevent items from being hidden in such containers, but will also reduce the amount of space needed to store them. If a trash or garbage shed is utilized, provisions should be made to lock these areas when they are not in use and to keep unauthorized persons from entering. Years ago when milk was delivered in bulk cans, it was an easy matter for an employee in collusion with the deliveryman to hide items in the milk cans, which were picked up each morning. Since the packaging of milk has changed, this situation may no longer exist, but it does point out that any time a container of any type leaves the premises, there is a possibility that it contains some stolen items. Hotel security must be alert to such possibilities and take the necessary precautions. Supervisors responsible for trash or garbage holding areas and trash removal should inspect these areas constantly.

Contract Services

Certain services within the hotel may be performed by outside contractors who enter the premises on a routine basis and who may be required to work in various locations throughout the building. These include, among others, window washers, exterminators, service personnel from utility companies, and maintenance men for elevators and other machinery. In addition, construction and decorating work may be done by outside contractors who may be in the building for days, weeks or months. These persons, like any other visitors, should be required to sign in and out. In addition, when any contract employee is likely to be working in areas where materials, supplies and personal property are readily available, the innkeeper should require that these persons be bonded by the contractor. A good example of such a case would be an outside window washing contractor. These window washers enter guest rooms as well as public spaces, and the opportunity for theft is very great. The innkeeper must also be certain that any outside contractor working in the hotel has sufficient liability insurance. The contractor should be required to file a certificate of this insurance with the innkeeper before he is permitted to work in the building.

Employees' Visitors

Many times friends or members of an employee's family will come to the hotel and request permission to see the employee. These persons should never be permitted to enter the hotel. If it appears that the request is an emergency of some type, the employee's supervisor should be notified. He can then decide whether the employee may be released from work and allowed to meet the caller at the service entrance. Under no circumstances, however, should the caller be allowed to enter the hotel and go to the employee.

Instances may occur when police or other officials may request permission to see an employee. Even if armed with a warrant, the official should not be permitted to enter the hotel's service area. The supervisor should be notified and requested to bring the employee to the service entrance or to a designated office, such as the personnel or security office. This will prevent confusion, embarrassment and possible dangerous situations from developing in front of other employees or guests.

OTHER PERIMETER OPENINGS

Emergency Exits

Service entrances may be operated on a 24-hour basis or may be open only during certain hours. They must be controlled when they are in operation. Aside from these entrances and exits, fire doors or emergency exits provide other means of egress and exit from the building. By law, these doors may not be locked if they are considered emergency exits. They normally cannot be opened from the outside and are equipped with panic hardware on the inside. Such doors must remain closed at all times and should be equipped with some type of alarm system that will indicate when they are opened.

Needless to say, such an alarm system must be monitored, and response to the alarm must be instantaneous. These doors must never be propped open to provide ventilation or for any other reason unless they are under constant supervision. It is quite apparent that an emergency door, if unattended and not provided with some form of alarm system, makes a perfect means of getting in or out of the building with stolen merchandise.

Life Safety and Security

Fire doors and fire towers are part of the life safety features of a building, but they also may provide a security feature. These stairs and towers provide a refuge, point of access, escape route, and often the scene of the crime itself for the murderer, rapist, mugger, robber and others intent upon criminal acts against the hotel or its occupants. To overcome the use of these facilities for illegal activities, we must ensure that they are used only for the emergency purposes intended.

It must be ensured that access cannot be obtained via these emergency exits. Fire stairways should not be considered and used as access stairs between occupied floors of the building. Arrangements can be made to provide keys or other devices to open such doors from the outside by the fire department; or magnetic systems can be employed which normally keep a door in a locked position but automatically open in a fire situation. Sensors in fire towers can alert security personnel to movement within the stairwell so they can investigate immediately.

It was an unguarded, unlocked, unprotected emergency fire door and stairway that permitted the assailant in the Howard Johnson's Hotel case to gain entry to the building. As indicated earlier, the use of these stairways by guests to leave the hotel undetected or with hotel property, or for employees to remove stolen property from the hotel, has been a concern of management for years. The ability to control such activities is available at no great expense and should be considered and implemented by every owner of a building with tenant-occupied facilities.

Security of Windows

Windows also present a problem, since stolen articles can be thrown or lowered from windows to persons outside the building. Naturally windows will have to be opened for ventilation, so it is not advisable in most situations to secure the window permanently. However, the installation of a good heavy screen or grille-work of some type will suffice, provided it is properly maintained. In some areas, such as food preparation rooms, it will be mandatory to have screens on the windows for insect control; in effect, the screen will serve two purposes.

If a grille of some type is used on a window, care should be taken that it cannot be opened from the inside, or can be opened only with a special key or tool. At the same time, the fire department should be able to open it from the outside. This is not required on ground level windows where it would not be advisable to have grilles that can be opened from the outside, but on upper floors the windows should be accessible to fire department personnel for ventilation or rescue operations.

Chapter 8

Alcoholic Beverage Service

INTERNAL SECURITY RESPONSIBILITY

Even if the hotel or motel feels it has succeeded in keeping out all undesirables, and believes all its employees are honest, such will never be the case. For any number of reasons, some people will steal, and the more opportunity they have, the more they will steal. An innkeeper who believes that *all* thefts are inevitable and must be considered part of the cost of doing business, however, must be educated to the facts. A few small items missing each day may not seem like much in dollars and cents, but over a period of time, reflected in annual inventory figures, these losses can amount to a staggering total. The margin of profit in the hotel industry is low enough as it is, and these losses represent money taken right out of profits. Every item that is stolen must be replaced; the more the innkeeper pays out, naturally, the less he has in the end. Therefore, it becomes an economic necessity to prevent losses, no matter how small the individual theft may be in dollars and cents.

Accountability Necessary

Just as physical security—locks, safes, steel doors, alarms, sensors, etc.—is important, so too is "paper" security—ledgers, log books, receiving and disbursing sheets, requisitions, inventory sheets and the like. Without some method of establishing accountability, there is no security. All the tools available to security, if they are not properly used and maintained, will be of little value. The most expensive lock in the world is only as good as the control of the key that opens it. Likewise, if accurate records are not maintained, checked and reviewed, the security program is compromised.

The security officer is concerned with this internal security, but responsibility also rests with department heads and with the accounting department. The more a security officer knows about the operations of each department, the better he will be able to perform his duties. The operations of each specific department, however, are the direct responsibility of that department head, and security within the department is part of the operation. We shall attempt to point out in this and the following chapters various areas where security must be maintained in each department so that the security officer may have some idea of where problems may occur.

THE ALCOHOLIC BEVERAGE SYSTEM

One of the most sensitive targets for theft in a hotel is the stock of alcoholic beverages. The reasons for this are:

1. The ease with which liquor can be clandestinely stolen by dishonest employees;
2. The ease of subsequent disposal and comparatively high resale value. If a thief steals jewelry, for example, it is unlikely that he can dispose of it for more than 30 percent of its retail value, whereas liquor can be resold for about 75 percent of its retail value.

Alcoholic beverages are vulnerable to removal in bulk, with or without the connivance of employees, by breaking and entering of stockrooms; and to removal by dishonest employees, usually in small quantities over a period of time. The aim of a security program is to make liquor stocks as difficult to steal as possible.

There are a number of ways that liquor can be stolen. Some of the more common methods are:

1. Thefts from stockrooms by employees or others.

2. Thefts from unattended bars.
3. Bar "padding." (This will be explained in detail later in this chapter.)
4. Fraudulent inventory checks.
5. Other fraud or theft involving beverages or cash receipts.
6. Fraudulent use of credit cards.

In order to understand how these thefts are accomplished, we must first review the alcoholic beverage system. While each establishment will have its own system, the variations are usually only minor details and the basic operation is as follows.

Placing and Receipt of Orders

Alcoholic beverages are ordered from the wholesaler by a purchasing officer, wine steward, or the food and beverage manager. At the time he places his order, it is recorded on an order blank specifying brand name, size of bottle, quantity and price. A copy of the completed order should be forwarded to the clerk in the receiving room where the material will be delivered.

Upon delivery, the material is checked in against the bill of lading to assure that what has been ordered is received. Quantities, brands and condition of merchandise should be checked carefully. If any cases have broken seals, they should be examined to ensure the proper number of bottles are enclosed, that there are no broken or open bottles. If a case appears to have been damaged, it can be weighed. Each case has the weight printed on the outside; if there has been any leakage, it can be noted by the discrepancy in weight. All of this must be accomplished before receipt of the goods is acknowledged. Following receipt, the merchandise should be placed in the liquor storeroom as soon as possible. During the time between receipt and storage, care must be taken to protect the merchandise, especially if loose bottles are involved.

When the material is stored in the liquor storeroom, it should be checked once again against the original order and against the bill of lading. If the order is correct, the bill of lading may be approved and forwarded to the proper office for payment. The merchandise is then placed in the stockroom according to type and brand for ease in counting and identifying. Some wines may require refrigeration, so provisions for cooling may be needed.

Stocking Bars

Normally bars are stocked with a predetermined quantity of each item. Each day, the bartender, wine steward, or whoever has been given the authority, gathers the empty bottles from the previous shift or day and orders replacements to replenish his stock. The quantities and items desired are listed on a beverage requisition sheet which is signed by the person ordering the goods. The requisition is then sent to the liquor stockroom, where the order is filled. The requisition is signed by the person filling the order and transported to the bar, where the merchandise is checked once again against the original order. If the goods received in the bar agree with the requisition, the requisition is again signed by the person in the bar receiving the goods. From this point on, the material is available for sale either by the drink or by the bottle, depending on the services offered by the particular bar, lounge or retail store. Whenever any liquor leaves the bar, a check or some accounting device must be given in exchange.

Reconciliation

At the close of a day's business, the checks will be added up, the sales on the cash register will be recorded, and the amount of liquor dispensed will be computed. This last requirement necessitates a physical inventory of liquor on hand. Full bottles are counted and open bottles are measured to determine remaining amounts. There are methods of comparing actual sales against potential sales, and it can be determined with reasonable accuracy if the operation is being run properly and honestly. When the actual cash or charges received do not support the quantity of liquor dispensed, the matter must be investigated. If the bar appears to be doing a great deal of business but the receipts and the amount of liquor dispensed do not appear to support the number of persons frequenting the bar, the matter must also be investigated. The accounting practices in effect are vital to support any security program. While the maintenance of these accounting practices is not the responsibility of the security officer, they are tools that make his job easier.

This briefly explains the operation of the beverage department in general. We can now apply those methods of stealing outlined previously and offer some suggestions on avoiding such thefts.

METHODS OF THEFT

Thefts from Stockrooms

From the time liquor is received until it is placed in the stockroom, it must not be left unattended unless it is under lock and key. If it is placed in a holding area, this must be a secure area with good locks. The keys to this lock should be minimal in number and strictly accounted for at all times. The person receiving the merchandise should be held accountable for it until it is turned over to the liquor storeroom custodian.

Alcoholic beverages should be stored separately from dry goods, produce and other supplies, in a location reserved for liquor only. The main alcoholic beverage storeroom should be a high-security area, equipped with a strong door (preferably metal) with the finest locking devices. It is desirable that this room have no windows and only one door. If this is not possible, heavy iron bars must be installed on the windows to prevent illegal entry.

As this room may contain many thousands of dollars' worth of alcoholic beverages, additional security is suggested by way of an intrusion alarm to detect any attempt to enter the area through walls, floors or ceilings. This suggestion is especially valid where one or more walls are outside walls. When such an alarm is provided, it must be carefully and continuously monitored, and when activated, it should bring immediate response.

Responsibility for this storage area should be placed in the hands of one individual who will be held accountable for the contents. Accordingly, there should be only two keys to the storage area—one held by the responsible custodian and one in the safe possession of the innkeeper for emergency use only. At no time should this area be left unlocked if unattended.

A physical inventory of the stockroom should be taken at least monthly, and a running inventory should be kept daily. A separate card should be provided for each item on hand, indicating purchases. Each day, the number of items issued from the stockroom should be posted from the bar requisitions, leaving a balance that should be on hand in the stockroom. The amount on hand according to the book should be physically checked against the amount counted in the stockroom. This will determine, if these figures do not agree, that merchandise has been removed from the stockroom without a requisition. This may be due to an error in counting, an issue not properly recorded, or a theft. In any event, if the figures do not agree, an investigation is certainly warranted.

Once the beverage is issued from the stockroom, it should be transported as quickly as possible to its final destination. Once again, it should never be left unattended. During this transporting procedure, liquor often disappears. Along the way the barboy transporting the goods can slip a few bottles of beer or a bottle of whisky to a fellow employee or hide it himself. If the person receiving the merchandise in the bar is careful to check his receipts before placing the liquor on the shelves or in the beer boxes, any shortage will be discovered and can be investigated immediately. If this check is not made by the receiving bartender, the barboy or whoever is responsible for transporting the liquor from the storeroom to the bar should be accompanied by a responsible person to prevent any losses en route.

Thefts from Unattended Bars

At no time should a bar be left unattended if open for business with the merchandise displayed for service. This holds true not only for public bars but also for service bars. If the bartender must leave for any reason, a responsible person should take his place. At no time should unauthorized persons be allowed behind the bar. If a bartender has to leave his station for any reason, a waiter or any other person should not be permitted to take his place unless authorized to do so by the innkeeper.

When the bar is closed for business, measures must be taken to secure the stock in a safe manner. A light screen or light wood panel over the shelves is not considered good security. Any unauthorized person can easily cut or break such a device. Since no two bars are the same, the methods of night storage will differ, so we can only recommend that every possible precaution be taken to ensure the safety of the merchandise. It is also recommended that some form of night light be provided so that an unauthorized person entering the bar will not have the cover of darkness in which to operate. Keys to the liquor cabinets or shelves must be accounted for carefully to assure that they do not fall into the hands of the potential thief. If a key is lost or disappears for a period of time, the locks should be changed immediately.

Bar "Padding"

Bar "padding" is a profitable method sometimes used by dishonest barmen. It should be watched for carefully, since it is sometimes hard to detect and sometimes even harder to prove. It involves the bartender providing his own bottle, selling its contents in the bar instead of using the hotel's stock, and pocketing the receipts of those sales. The tip-off of such practice normally is where there appears to be a good number of customers in the bar, but the cash receipts and amount of liquor sold do not appear to support the volume of activity. One fifth may serve 17 drinks, which might net the bartender $12.00 or so. This would not appear as a big difference in cash sales, but any greater quantity of bootleg liquor would begin to make a difference.

Liquor brought from the outside can find its way to the bar in many ways. If there is no inspection of incoming packages at the service entrance, as we have mentioned, the bartender or anyone he is working with can carry the goods right into the hotel. If there is an outside entrance to the bar from the street, the bartender or anyone working with him can merely walk in off the street with a package and deposit it behind the bar. The methods for getting the illegal alcohol to the bartender are numerous, and it is the security officer's duty to prevent such activity.

To assist in identifying stock not belonging to the hotel, each bottle of hotel liquor is sometimes marked with an indelible code number or some form of stamp before it leaves the stockroom. This marking need not be obvious, except to those who are required to know its location or existence. In this manner, the investigator can determine at a glance if any given bottle is from hotel stock or has been brought in from the outside.

If a bartender is aware of this coding system, he could pour the contents of "his" bottle into an empty marked bottle. While this pouring from one bottle to another should not be allowed and is in violation of the law, the bartender is not always under direct supervision. Many things can and do happen that are against hotel policy and are illegal.

All empty liquor bottles should be retained in a given place so that they can be counted following the close of a shift or the day's business. In many areas, returnable beer and soft drink bottles are used for which a return is paid by the bottler. Care must be taken that these returnable empties are salvaged and separated from the "throw-aways." Control of these empties must be maintained to ensure collection of the deposit by the licensee.

The replenishment requisition is made up based on the "empties," and it is also a way to check for non-coded bottles. If any liquor bottles are found in other than the required depository, such as a trash barrel, it should be determined why this empty was not placed with the others. Bar "padding" can be a serious problem, so care should be maintained to use every means possible to prevent such action.

Fraudulent Inventory Checks

Fraudulent inventory checks can cover serious deficiencies and can also cause serious problems. If the bartender or anyone connected with the operation of the bar is entrusted with taking the inventory, the records can be falsified to cover shortages. Therefore, it is of the utmost importance that those charged with the taking of inventories not be the same people responsible for the bar operation.

Full bottles with the seals unbroken are easy to count. A difficulty occurs in computing the remaining amounts in open bottles. Various gauges are available, normally based on tenths, which will measure the contents when held alongside the bottle. Bottles come in various shapes and sizes, so more than one gauge may be necessary. For an absolutely accurate measurement, the contents would have to be poured out into a measuring glass and then returned to the original container. This is time-consuming and in one case led to an unfortunate allegation. This method was used to measure partial bottles, and after each measurement the glass measure was rinsed with clear water. One particular bottle which was seldom used was subject to this treatment daily for a period of time. Finally a drink was served from this bottle. The customer complained that the drink was diluted, and an allegation was made that the bartender was watering the liquor. An investigation proved that, over a period of time, the excess water in the measuring glass, just a drop a day, was sufficient to dilute the liquor. Consequently, if a measure is used to determine amounts in open bottles, it must be completely dry when in use.

This story points up the problem of liquor being diluted accidentally or intentionally. Often employees having access to liquor supplies will cover the theft of a drink by adding the same amount of water to the bottle. Thus the theft is not noted until the liquor becomes so diluted that a customer complains, or until a test is made of the liquor with a hydrometer and the dilution is discovered. If dilution appears to be a possible problem, a hydrometer should be purchased and spot checks made on bottles at regular intervals.

It is the authors' opinion that gauges held alongside the bottle, or the practiced eye of the inventory taker, are sufficiently accurate. Regardless of the shape of the bottle, it is not too difficult to determine whether it is half full, one quarter full, or what have you, based on tenths. The important thing is that, once inventory figures have been taken, they should be related to sales so that if there is an apparent difference, it can be checked immediately.

Other Fraud or Theft Involving Beverages or Cash

No one could identify all the methods used to steal merchandise or money from the hotel or bar. Every day, waiters, bartenders, other employees and customers find new ways to beat the system. It is mandatory that certain policies designed to prevent such stealing be set forth and strictly enforced. Since the security officer plays a part in seeing that such policies are adhered to, he must be well aware of the rules and regulations. Such rules may include, but certainly not be limited to, the following:

1) *The previous employment records* of bartenders, cocktail waiters or waitresses, or any person handling alcoholic beverages, should be carefully checked before hiring. Consideration should also be given to bonding such employees. If extra employees are required for short periods of time, they should be closely supervised by a responsible person.

2) *The size of the drink to be served* must be determined and

the bartender should be required to use a proper size "shot glass" or "line glass." "Shot glasses" can be deceptive by the use of "loaded bottoms" or other tricks that make the glass appear to hold more than it actually does. The accuracy of the measure, whether it be an ounce, ounce-and-a-half, or whatever, is sometimes questioned.

Accurate measures can be secured in plain glass or what is referred to as a "line glass." A plain glass calibrated to measure one ounce is constructed so that, when filled to the brim, it holds one ounce. A line glass will have a line etched in the glass itself that indicates the required amount has been poured when filled to that line. There is still unused glass above the line.

The line glass is considered by many to be more efficient, since there is less spillage. In addition, if the licensee wishes, a one-ounce line glass may be used and the bartender instructed to pour over the line. In this way, the customer feels he is getting a larger drink, while the licensee has already determined that he is going to serve one-and-a-half ounces per drink. The glass filled to the brim would not exceed the desired quantity.

For those concerned with the possible inaccuracies of shot glasses, other measuring devices are available. Automatic dispensing machines are available which dispense the required amount of liquor as well as counting the number of drinks taken from the bottle. It cannot be pointed out too strongly that this system is not infallible. The authors have seen cases where the mechanism has been altered so that a larger drink is dispensed and the count is inaccurate.

At any rate, *some* facility must be provided to accurately measure the amount of liquor disbursed in order to maintain control—*quality* as well as *quantity* control.

3) *A check must be provided for each drink* at the time it is served. This is not to say that many drinks cannot appear on one check, but each drink should be recorded on the check as it is served. If the guest is at the bar, the check should be placed in front of him. If the guest is seated at a table and being served by a waitress, the waitress may carry the check or leave it with the cashier or checker.

Just how checks are to be handled is of vital importance, as there are many systems that can be worked by the "sharp" waiter or waitress. Checks should be signed for to prevent loss and establish accountability. When a check is paid, it should be rung into the register immediately. It should be determined ahead of time who is to price the checks, total them and record them in the machine. There are various methods available, all of which serve a purpose and have good aspects as well as drawbacks. The policy to be followed will depend a great deal on existing circumstances, type of clientele, number of employees, layout of area, etc.

One favorite trick involves a waiter who is serving several parties, all of whom have had several drinks. One party calls for their check, but the waiter presents the check of another party who has consumed more drinks. For example, instead of presenting the party its check for $10.50, the waiter presents another party's check for $12.00. If the customer balks and claims this is not his check, the waiter can plead his error and present the proper check. If the customer does not examine the check but merely pays the amount shown, the waiter is home clear. He turns in the $10.50 check to the cashier together with $10.50 in cash, and pockets the extra $1.50. He still has the $12.00 check to present to the proper party when the time comes. Once the correct $12.00 check is paid, the waiter may keep it to be used on still another party later in the evening.

Requiring checks to be left with a cashier until they are called for to be paid, and then to be returned to the cashier immediately, can control this method of cheating the customer.

4) *Beverages must be served and handled only by designated employees.* Waiters and others should not be permitted to "help themselves" but should be served by a bartender who must see a check before issuing a drink. Payment for these drinks must be accounted for.

5) *Free drinks should not be given,* regardless of how good a customer might be. If management desires to give a customer a free drink, a representative of management should purchase the drink, receive a check covering its cost, and properly sign the check, indicating who is being entertained. As stated before, *every* drink served must be covered by a check.

6) *Bartender or cashier banks should be checked frequently* to assure that no shortages or overages are being covered. Banks should be kept to a minimum amount necessary to transact business. If business is particularly heavy, excess cash should be removed prior to the end of a shift. Each bartender should have

his own bank, and no one should be permitted to use another's bank.

Dishonest Bartender Practices

These are only a few suggestions of security measures that can be applied. There are some methods of stealing that cannot be planned against, such as:

- The bartender who, in wiping the top of the bar, accidentally "sweeps away" some loose change that was lying in front of a customer.
- The bartender who, when business is at a peak and the bar is crowded, gives incorrect change intentionally, hoping the customer will not notice.
- The bartender who collects from two members of the same party when things are busy enough to cover his actions.
- The bartender who pours short, getting more than the required number of drinks from a bottle, pocketing the money received for that extra drink or two.
- The bartender who takes care of his friends with an occasional free drink in order to get a bigger tip.

It is far more difficult to protect the guest from a dishonest bartender or waiter than to protect the hotel against the same person. Constant supervision of the bartenders by the department head, management and the security officer is required. In addition, undercover agents or "shills," as they are sometimes referred to, may be used. Such persons, unknown to the bartenders, frequent the bar and observe what takes place, reporting any infractions of hotel policy or law to management.

Padding the Bill for Parties

Another situation sometimes develops which bears consideration. It is the case where a customer becomes the victim of a conspiracy that may or may not have the approval of management. We would prefer to believe that the innkeeper would never resort to such a fraud; it may arise from a desire on the part of certain employees to increase their portion of a tip while securing alcoholic beverages for themselves. The operation is as follows:

Liquor is sometimes sold on a bottle basis for parties taking place in the hotel. The cost per bottle sometimes includes the cost of mixes, garnishes, ice and service. The price is therefore relatively high, but if all the components were charged for separately, the total might well be higher. Following the function, the number of bottles consumed is calculated and the cost computed.

The customer may not get an honest count on the number of bottles consumed. Dishonest employees may remove full bottles and replace them with empties, or, if the customer does not bother to count his full bottles and his empties, the total can be increased merely by adding additional bottles to the bill. Since the gratuity charged is normally a percentage of the total bill, it can be seen that the gratuity will be increased also.

Unless the innkeeper condones such an operation, it should be made abundantly clear to all headwaiters, wine stewards, barmen and others who may be involved in accounting for merchandise consumed, that such a practice of "padding" the bill will not be tolerated. It then becomes incumbent upon the security officer to assist in the enforcement of this directive. It should be brought to the customer's attention that he has a right to count the bottles available at the beginning of a function. If he desires, he may mark the bottles in any manner he pleases for easy identification. At the close of the party he also has the right to inspect and count all empties and to settle with management on charges for the amount actually consumed.

The customer also has the right to insist that no additional liquor be brought to the bar in excess of his original order without his express permission. In this way, if the function is a big success and more liquor is required than was anticipated, the client has the right to make his own decision as to providing additional liquor. If the matter is not handled in this manner, an unscrupulous wine steward may add additional bottles (empties), stating that the bar was running low and additional liquor was required. True, this increases the hotel's profits, but normally the person perpetrating such a fraud does not have the interest of the hotel at heart but is looking to increase his share of the gratuity. This is a vicious fraud and it is hoped that no respectable hotel owner or innkeeper would ever be a party to such a practice.

Fraudulent Use of Credit Cards

This is a common practice today where the customer is committing a fraud upon the innkeeper. It is a very difficult crime to prevent, especially in a transient location such as a bar. If the credit card has a space where the bearer is required to sign his or her name, this signature should be checked against the customer's signature on the bar check or credit card voucher. If there is a discrepancy, the matter should be investigated. If it is felt that the card may be stolen or invalid, most major credit card companies maintain a 24-hour, toll-free telephone service to check the validity of credit cards. If necessary, this service should be used without hesitation. Credit card companies also publish cancellation bulletins of invalid cards.

Some independent hotels issue their own credit cards as a convenience to their better customers and to business people in the area. Where such a system exists, a record of current cards should be kept at each cashier's location so that a given card can be immediately verified. Such a record can be kept on a roll-type card file capable of holding over a thousand individual names.

Objectives of Alcoholic Beverage Security

It is difficult at best to obtain an exact reconciliation of cash against liquor dispensed, due to allowances that must be made for spillage and for mixed drinks which may vary in consistency. However, consistent shortages or differences should be investigated.

The objective of security in regard to alcoholic beverage service is to maintain a situation in which the stock is secure and where liquor disposed of is equated by cash receipt or some other token of value. In order to accomplish these objectives, we must have honest employees, we must provide proper security for our stockrooms and bars, we must ensure that only designated persons shall handle alcoholic beverages, and we must ensure that accountability controls are maintained at all times. This requires the combined efforts of management, department heads and the security officer in varying degrees of supervision. In any department of the hotel, if an employee knows that no one is checking on him, his production or operation, he will feel free to do as he pleases. Again, if the opportunity to steal is removed, part of the battle has been won.

LAWS GOVERNING ALCOHOLIC BEVERAGES

The security officer must also be concerned with the hotel's adherence to laws governing the sale of liquor.

There are probably no more stringent laws and regulations affecting hotels than those involved with the sale and service of alcoholic beverages. The industry is governed by an authority, whether it be the Liquor License Board, the Alcoholic Beverage Commission, or some other group with a different title, which obtains its authority from State, Provincial or Federal statutes. Enforcement is normally absolute, strict and continuous. Licenses are issued in a limited number permitting the sale of liquor, and the issue of such a license obligates the licensee to comply with all rules and regulations or risk loss of the license. "Ignorance of the law" is absolutely no excuse or defense in a violation of the liquor laws. The rules and regulations may differ from area to area, but there are certain regulations that are common to all liquor statutes. The security officer should be familiar with them.

Age Limit

There is an age limit on the service or sale of alcoholic beverages. In some states it is 21 years of age, while other states have lower ages as the minimum. Whatever the age limit, sale to an underage patron is a violation of the law. The fact that the patron lied about his age is no defense, unless the patron signed an affidavit stating his age which was witnessed by a third party prior to the sale of the beverage. Driver's licenses and other identification have not been accepted in some jurisdictions as legal proof of age. The law even goes to the extreme of saying that if liquor is purchased for on-premises consumption by an adult for a minor, the innkeeper can still be held liable. Thus, if Mom orders a martini for her 15-year-old daughter, service should be refused.

Sales to Intoxicated Patrons

Another regulation prohibits the sale of alcoholic beverages to an intoxicated person. If a patron who appears to be intoxicated orders a drink or attempts to purchase a bottle for off-premises consumption, service should be refused. This calls for a judgment on the part of the seller. Some instances will be relatively easy to determine, while others will be more difficult, since different people react differently when "under the influence." The law in fact states that where alcohol is being served for immediate consumption, the patron should not be allowed to get intoxicated. If a patron becomes intoxicated, leaves the bar, goes into the street and injures a third party or himself, the innkeeper will be held liable and may lose his license.

Although the legal definition of "under the influence" differs from area to area, the amount of alcohol in the blood is actually very small in most cases, so it behooves bar operators to be aware of the consumption of their patrons. It becomes a ticklish situation at best, as a bartender does not like to "flag" a patron unless it is absolutely necessary in order to maintain order. The law, however, is strict and penalties are severe.

Quality of Liquor Served

A third serious condition set forth in the alcoholic beverage regulations concerns what is being served. It is not permissible to refill empty liquor bottles nor to pour the contents of one bottle into another. Periodic field tests will be conducted to determine the proof of the liquor in a given bottle. If, for any reason, the proof does not come up to that stated on the label, the licensee will be held guilty. There have been a number of cases where this has occurred. One such case demonstrates what can happen and how, and what the results will be.

A night cleaner in a bar made a practice of sneaking a drink from one particular bottle each night. To cover his theft, he added an equal amount of water to the bottle. Naturally this was all done without the knowledge of the bartender or the licensee. A field investigator from the beverage commission made a routine inspection, and the tampered bottle happened to be one he chose to test. What was supposed to be 86 proof liquor naturally was nowhere near 86 proof after the addition of the water, and the licensee was cited for a violation. The result was a suspension of the license for 30 days in spite of the fact that a defense was offered stating the licensee had no knowledge of what had taken place.

An inn, restaurant or bar which has its license suspended for 30 days loses a great deal of business, not only the bar business itself but related business as well. For example, if a convention was due to come into the hotel and its sponsors were informed that no liquor could be served while they were in attendance, they might consider moving their convention elsewhere.

Comprehensive Regulations

The regulations covering alcoholic beverage service set forth by the controlling agencies are too numerous to cover completely in this text. Suffice it to say they cover every aspect of the operation: advertising, promotions, give-away programs, entertainment, service, purchasing, facilities, location, hours, patron conduct, as well as specifications as to who is entitled to secure a license. It is of the utmost importance that every security officer be familiar with the rules and regulations of the liquor control board or commission in his own licensing area, and it is most important that the security officer ensure that these regulations are adhered to absolutely.

The protection of the patron, not only from others but from himself as well, becomes a more vital matter in a bar as compared to a dining room or restaurant. A licensee is not required to prevent a patron from *eating* too much, but he is required to prevent him from *drinking* too much. This restriction extends to room service also. If a guest orders a bottle of liquor sent to his room, this would appear to be within reason. However, if he should order several bottles a day and it is obvious that he is not entertaining but consuming all the liquor himself, the service should be discontinued.

Another situation requiring caution occurs when an intoxicated guest calls for his car with the intention of driving away. The guest should be prevented from driving if he appears at all impaired. If a controversy develops where the guest insists he is fit to drive and insists the hotel give him the keys to his car, it is better to call the local police and detain the guest until the police arrive. Let the police observe the guest and take the necessary steps to prohibit his driving. If such action is not taken, any injury or damage the impaired driver may cause or suffer will be blamed on the innkeeper who allowed him to drive, knowing he was intoxicated.

It is obvious that, under such conditions as we have outlined, continuous supervision must be extended over all the beverage service throughout the licensed property. (See Appendixes for sample liquor control acts.)

Chapter 9

The Food Service Department

From a profit-making point of view, food is not as attractive a theft target as cash or liquor, but this does not prevent it from being stolen continually. The current high cost of food makes it an eminently stealable commodity. Most theft of food in a hotel is committed by employees sporadically as opportunity arises. If this practice becomes well established in a hotel, the economic loss resulting over a period of time will be considerable. In general, control measures are largely a matter of common sense and will vary in detail according to local conditions. Areas where the threat of theft or loss of food may occur include:

1. Theft of food by, or with the connivance of, employees.
2. Undercharging customers for food served.
3. Waste by incompetence or malpractice on the part of kitchen staff.
4. Lack of policy and/or supervision regarding the disposal of surplus foods.
5. Lack of control of garbage disposal.
6. Dishonest buying practices.
7. Unsatisfactory production and portion control.
8. Waste of food by overbuying due to inaccurate forecast of needs.

THE FOOD SERVICE OPERATION

The hotel food department is a complex operation, and it is difficult to separate good catering and management practices from security. A discussion of food security must involve these other practices to a degree, and it is hoped that a better understanding of the entire food service operation will assist the security officer in realizing his obligations and duties. Let us outline briefly what might be considered an average food department operation, bearing in mind that many minor differences may occur in any given operation.

Purchasing Specifications

Foodstuffs and materials used in the food department are purchased by a purchasing steward, purchasing officer, chef, other authorized person or any combination of such persons. It is desirable that purchasing specifications be established in advance and published for all concerned. For example, although a rib of beef may seem to the uninformed to be just a rib of beef, ribs come in a number of qualities, weights, sizes and degrees of trim. A decision must be made in advance exactly which rib is the most economical for the hotel to use. Eggs are eggs, but they can be small, medium or large, brown or white, fresh or frozen, and it must be determined exactly what is to be purchased. The same holds true for every item purchased for use in the food department. Without definite specifications, economic control and standardization of products cannot be ensured.

Assuming that specifications have been established, materials are ordered from selected purveyors. The purveyors also must be aware of the specifications so that when they quote a price on a given item, each purveyor is quoting on exactly the same item. The buyer decides which purveyor will get the order; the order is written and a copy sent to the receiving clerk.

Checking Deliveries

When the items are delivered, they must be carefully checked against the original order. They must also be checked to determine if they meet the hotel's specifications. Items purchased by the pound, such as meats, should be weighed to ensure that weight delivered agrees with weight billed. Produce must be checked for freshness, quality and amount. The receiving clerk is responsible for ensuring that only such items as meet specifications are accepted by the hotel, and that only items that have been ordered are accepted.

If the shipment is acceptable, the receiving clerk acknowledges receipt and the goods are placed in the appropriate storage areas—fresh produce under refrigeration, frozen articles in freezers, and dry goods in clean, dry storage. Accountability for the merchandise now rests with the receiving clerk or storeroom manager, as the case may be, and this accountability will remain with him until the goods are dispersed to others.

Requisitioning

Goods from the storerooms are only dispersed upon receipt of a written requisition signed by an authorized person. Food may be ordered out for the cooks by the chef; for the pantry by the pantry manager, etc.; or all food may be requisitioned only by the supervising chef. This is a matter of individual policy agreed upon by management, but once it is decided who has the authority to requisition goods, no exceptions should be made. If every kitchen worker is allowed to write his own requisitions, there is no control or supervision over what is being ordered and no assurance that the items ordered are being used in the kitchen production.

Accountability in Kitchen

Once the material is requisitioned to the kitchen, accountability passes to the proper authority there. The material may be stored in the kitchen and ultimately will be used in the production of meals or in the operation of the kitchen. Foodstuffs and other supplies must be kept under lock and key and/or close supervision. Storage boxes should not be left open and unattended. Key control again is vital to ensure the safety of stored items. Unauthorized personnel should not be allowed in the kitchen area, and waiters and waitresses should not be permitted in the working areas. This rule should be strictly enforced at all times.

Goods brought to the kitchen are prepared for sale to the customer or are used in the production of goods to be sold. The most economic use possible should be attained in this preparation. Following preparation, accountability again changes hands when the waiter or waitress presents an order to be served to a guest. No food item should leave the kitchen unless there is a proper food check covering it. Cash is received for items sold, thereby completing the food service operation.

Ideally, every item prepared is sold by the end of the day, but of course this is never the case. Leftovers should be properly stored and protected for future use. Unusable portions of goods are disposed of as garbage.

Let us take one item—say a canned ham—and follow it through the basic stages of the food service operation. Once the ham is delivered to the hotel, one of the following conditions must exist:

1. It is in the hands of the receiving clerk, stored in his storeroom; or
2. It is in the kitchen, stored in an appropriate holding area; or
3. There are food checks covering the sale of the ham or a part of it, in which case the remaining portion should be in storage as leftovers or as unprepared goods.

Many items are not sold directly but are used in production of other foodstuffs or as complementary ingredients. Examples are salt and pepper, sauces, condiments, cream, sugar, etc. Because there will not be any checks to cover the expenditure of these items, it is more difficult to maintain control. Here good catering practices, adequate supervision, and careful production controls become vital.

Records and Inventories

As in the case of beverages, adequate records must be maintained constantly and inventories are required. Food cost is computed by determining the cost of food used as compared to sales less the cost of labor. This is a vital figure to management in determining the success of the entire operation. An innkeeper who does not know what his food and labor costs amount to is operating in a void that could spell economic disaster. Menu prices cannot be established satisfactorily if these costs are not known and taken into consideration. Therefore, care must be taken to ensure that any accounting system used is maintained to the fullest and reviewed periodically to ensure the system is doing what it was designed to do.

Let us now discuss the specific threats previously mentioned and possible preventive measures.

METHODS OF FOOD THEFT

Food is easily and frequently stolen by employees, some of whom appear to think that taking food is some kind of fringe benefit which the hotel should admit and accept. Employee stealing of food normally occurs in one of two ways—the small theft that occurs on the spot and is consumed immediately, or the theft of some larger item that is hidden and later removed from the premises. If employee theft is prevalent, the food operation will soon show a loss instead of a profit.

Eating on the Spot

Even the most honest employee is sometimes tempted to "snitch" a piece of bacon or a slice of chicken or an apple to eat immediately. Eating on the spot can be controlled only by keeping the food out of reach of the employees (this is impractical in some cases) and by proper supervision. Kitchen stewards should be instructed that preventing this type of theft is part of their responsibility. Years ago, employees caught eating food were charged the cost of the items consumed, and this amount was deducted from their weekly pay. With the advent of labor unions and developments in social and civil rights, this practice is no longer permitted. Continual stealing of this type should result in some disciplinary action, after consultation with the appropriate labor union officials if necessary.

Stealing Food for Later Use

Taking food for later use is far more serious and usually involves a greater monetary value. Precautions to prevent this type of stealing include proper security of the items so they are not readily available to the employee; proper supervision of the work area; and close and careful inspection of work areas to prevent items from being hidden. Such stealing is often a cooperative arrangement, with a cook or storeroom clerk securing the item and hiding it until it can be passed along to a confederate.

Supervisors should always be on the alert for hidden items. In the process of inspecting working areas for cleanliness, supervisors have not only the right but the obligation to look in drawers, closets and other potential hiding places. We have already mentioned in a previous chapter the inspection of all packages leaving the building, the use of screens on windows, the right to search lockers and automobiles parked on the hotel premises, and the close supervision of the conduct of all employees. In addition, the hotel's policy should be made clear to all employees. They should be reminded by every means possible that such thefts will not be tolerated and that, if apprehended, the thief will be subject to prosecution. Management must keep its word in this manner; if a thief is apprehended, full prosecution should be undertaken and publicized. Some may disagree, but we believe the threat of punishment is a deterrent to crime.

While statistics can be misleading, they can also be enlightening. It has been determined by several independent studies that "old-time" employees are more likely to steal on the job than newcomers. They have had more time to figure out the system, they are friendly with everyone, their seniority allows them to take certain privileges that would not be afforded the newer man. Consequently, stealing is much easier. Trusted employees are those who steal; employees not trusted are not given an opportunity to steal. Nothing—age, length of service, sex, color—should influence the degree of supervision afforded an employee, or the decision to prosecute for a crime.

Undercharging Customers

Normally this practice is not too widespread. When it occurs it is usually due to incompetence rather than dishonesty. In either case, the hotel stands to lose. A waiter may undercharge in order to "take care of a friend," or hope for a larger tip due to his generosity to a guest. Such activities can be controlled if a cashier or checker is employed who will be responsible for the pricing and totalling of checks and handling all money. The dishonest practice discussed in Chapter 8 relative to bar service, where a more costly check is presented for payment in place of the proper check and the waiter pockets the excess cash, is sometimes attempted with food service as well.

Need for Duplicate Orders

Care should be taken that the cooks are given some type of order form that they may retain, showing the item being ordered. These duplicates, or "dupes" as they are referred to in the industry, can be compared against the actual food checks to ascertain that all items ordered were served and paid for. If a waiter turns in a "dupe" for a steak and a review of his checks reveals that he did not serve any steak, an investigation is warranted.

Waste in Preparation

This area is solely the responsibility of food service authorities. Waste in production can only be due to incompetence or poor supervision, both factors under the direct control of the chef or other responsible food service personnel. The economic loss can be great if such waste is permitted to continue.

In our list of threats of theft or loss of food, we included "lack of policy and/or supervision regarding disposal of surplus foods"; "unsatisfactory production and portion control"; and "waste of food by overbuying due to inaccurate forecast of needs." These forms of waste are areas over which the security officer has no direct control. It would be ideal if only the quantity of food to be actually sold was prepared, but this is not possible to plan precisely. Buying and preparation are usually done on the basis of forecasts of business expected. If these forecasts are incorrect for any reason, the results can be disastrous.

When there is surplus food, it should be cared for in a satisfactory manner so that some of the potential value can be recovered. The food may be used in future dishes (for example, leftover chicken might be used in chicken salad), it may be used to feed employees who are entitled to eat meals as part of their employment contract, or it may be made available for sale to employees at cost.

The keeping of production records is important so that menu planners and the chef can judge from past history what to expect by way of demand for any item under any set of circumstances. Overbuying can sometimes be handled by advance preparation and freezing the item for future use. Most of the results of waste will finally appear in one place—the garbage—and this is where the security officer can play a part in control of food losses.

Control of Garbage

Anyone checking on the efficiency of a kitchen operation will look first at the garbage generated by that kitchen. Any chef worthy of his position will keep a close watch on the garbage, and it behooves a security officer to do likewise—not only so that he can report any apparent increase in waste, but because garbage containers are ideal places for hiding and transferring foodstuffs and other stolen items to the outside. This may be done by employees in collusion with the garbage collector or contractor. Food wrapped in grease-proof paper and placed in a trash or garbage container can easily be smuggled out of the hotel for later pick-up. For this reason, security officers should make a point of inspecting garbage and trash receptacles as part of their normal routine.

The loss of silverware through garbage can be a big problem if care is not exercised on the table where dirty dishes are scraped. If large losses of flatware are being experienced, arrangements should be made to have the garbage from the dish table spread out and raked over in search of silverware.

Dishonest Buying Practices

Purchasing is an area where the profits to the thief can be great and the loss to management severe. There are a number of ways fraud or theft can take place. Purveyors can "short-weight" deliveries or substitute poorer quality merchandise than that ordered while charging the full top price. If, as we suggested earlier, specifications are established for all items and all items are weighed upon delivery, the purveyor will be unable to practice this fraud unless he is in collusion with the receiving clerk. This is a possibility, with the clerk receiving a payoff for his part in the fraud. Supervision of the receiving clerk and the storerooms will uncover substitutions in quality, although it might be more difficult to prove short weight once the items have been stored in the holding boxes and mixed with other merchandise.

There is still another form of fraud practiced whereby the hotel purchaser favors one purveyor over another regardless of price. For this preferential treatment, the buyer naturally receives a fee which may be considered a "kickback" or gratuity. If possible, buying from just one purveyor should be avoided, if all other elements are equal—price, quality, delivery, etc. Spreading the business around keeps all purveyors honest and "on their toes." In the event of shortages or emergencies, the hotel has several sources from which to draw. If management discovers all purchases are being made from one supplier, the matter should be investigated to determine if "kickbacks" are being made or if organized crime has infiltrated the purchasing department or influenced the buyer. (Organized crime as it pertains to the hotel industry will be discussed in Chapter 17.)

LAWS AFFECTING RESTAURANT OPERATIONS

For legal purposes the term "restaurant" includes coffee shops, public cafeterias, tea rooms, taverns, clubs or any other establishments which serve food to guests and/or to the public.

There are a number of federal, provincial, state and local laws that affect food operations. For the most part, these laws are concerned with the protection of the consumer and deal with such subjects as types of food served, sanitation, protection of brand names, health regulations, etc. Most restaurants are subject to inspections by local and/or higher authorities. The cleanliness of a restaurant is under the control of legal agencies who have the power to close any establishment not maintaining minimum standards. These standards normally will cover subjects such as storage of perishable foods, rodent and insect control, washroom facilities, general housekeeping, warewashing procedures, shellfish purchasing and inspection. In addition, there are laws such as the Oleomargarine Act, which is intended to protect the consumer from being deceived by the use of oleomargarine in place of butter.

While the operation of the restaurant and the preparation of foods is not the direct responsibility of the security officer, his knowledge of the legal obligations connected with such an operation is an asset in ensuring that requirements are met for the protection of the patron and the innkeeper.

Unfit Food

Perhaps the greatest danger in any food operation is the possibility of serving unfit food which may cause harm, such as food which is spoiled in some manner, or food containing some foreign object capable of causing injury. When an injury or illness does occur, the injured party is ready to lay the blame at the feet of the innkeeper or restaurant operator. If a person eats a meal and later that night becomes ill, naturally the victim will claim that the food most recently eaten caused his illness. "Ptomaine poisoning" is almost a standard claim for anyone who gets sick after eating in a restaurant. The difference between an upset stomach and ptomaine poisoning is usually the difference between life and death; real ptomaine poisoning usually comes close to being fatal. The fact that he drank too much liquor, followed by a large quantity of rich or strange foods, never enters the mind of the victim as a possible cause for his illness.

Investigating Claims of Illness

A security officer investigating a claim of illness due to eating certain food should attempt to secure as much information as possible, including, although not limited to, the following:

1. When did the victim become ill? (Date and hour.)
2. What was the nature of the illness? (Pains, vomiting, dizziness, etc.)
3. How long did the illness continue?
4. Was a doctor consulted or any medicine taken? If a doctor was consulted, a copy of his findings should be secured.
5. What food or foods does the victim claim caused his illness?
6. Why does he feel that these foods caused the illness? Did they have a particular odor, taste or appearance that caused suspicion?
7. What activities did the victim engage in prior to eating

the suspected foods? Had he been to any parties, consumed any alcohol, medicine? Had he been in the company of any other persons? If so, get names and addresses so they may be contacted for statements.

8. Had the victim sustained any traumatic experience prior to eating? If so, get full details.

9. If the victim is unable to pinpoint any particular item of food that is suspicious, secure a complete list of all food eaten.

10. Check hotel records (restaurant records) as to number of servings of each item consumed by the victim that were served that day.

11. Check records for any other reports of illnesses on that particular day.

While the human body differs in its ability to withstand certain conditions, and what might make one person ill will have no effect on another, it is certain that if food is served containing the ptomaine bacteria, more than one person will become ill. If 500 orders of a certain item are served at the dinner, it is relatively safe to assume that if that product was in some way "bad," more than one person would be affected. In the case of certain shellfish or other seafood, it is possible there could be one tainted item out of 500 or 1,000 that could cause illness to the person consuming it. That is why it is so important to know exactly what the victim consumed.

In the authors' experience, literally hundreds of claims have been presented for injuries claimed to have been caused by "bad" food, but never has one been found to be legitimate in the eyes of the courts. In most cases we were able to show what might be considered contributing factors such as mentioned previously—a quantity of alcohol consumed prior to eating, nervous tension or excitement, unusual quantities of food consumed, or eating in a hurry, all of which could and, in the eyes of the courts, apparently did have a contributing effect. Without proper investigation of the claims, however, we would never have been able to present our defense.

The case of a foreign object in food is a slightly different situation. Normally the innkeeper is made aware of the situation immediately. A person in the process of eating comes across a foreign object. Perhaps he chips a tooth, cuts or injures his mouth in some manner. He immediately registers a complaint with the waiter or management. Once again, all of the facts in the case must be secured and recorded for future use. Naturally, where injury is severe, immediate medical attention should be provided.

Today, the service of food in a hotel or restaurant is considered a sale with an implied warranty that the food is fit for human consumption. If the food is found to be unfit, there has been a breach of warranty and the injured party is entitled to recover damages. Some courts have held a different opinion, however, holding that the liability for serving unfit food is based on common law negligence. Regardless of what opinion is held, the fact remains that the innkeeper does not wish to serve food that is unfit, either by reason of spoilage or by the presence of foreign objects in it. In the event such an incident does take place, the innkeeper should have all the facts available to offer in defense.

Customers' Lost Property

If customers check personal belongings with restaurant management and management accepts custody of the items, management will be held responsible for their loss. If the patron hangs his coat on a hook on the wall and his coat disappears, there is no liability on the part of the management. The innkeeper is responsible to provide for the safety and comfort of the patron, but he is not responsible for the patron's personal effects.

SUMMARY

It might be said that there are three "golden rules" that must be observed in the food department if security is to be maintained.

1. Food suppliers or purveyors supplying the hotel, whether wholesale or retail, must be thoroughly reputable and must agree to meet the specifications set forth by hotel management.
2. Employees must be honest, well-trained and properly instructed in their duties and responsibilities; they must know that incompetence and violations of hotel policy will result in some form of disciplinary action.

3. Trash and garbage contractors must be supervised when removing materials from the hotel.

It must be appreciated that the food operation is an important area from a security standpoint and that the innkeeper is wise to give it the attention it deserves. There is a wide range of fraudulent practices connected with this operation and we have touched on only a few in this discussion. Such practices, and the preventive measures required to overcome them, will be dictated largely by local circumstances, size of hotel, and location. This makes it impossible to do more than generalize and to indicate certain areas that deserve attention. Close supervision by management will provide the best possible security.

Chapter 10

The Housekeeping Department

While the food and beverage service departments may be considered two of the greatest security risks within a hotel and subject to a high rate of stealing and fraud, there are other departments where stealing can be widespread and security considerations are equally important.

In addition to the duties of caring for guests' sleeping accommodations normally associated with the housekeeping department, there are other functions and what might be considered sub-departments. The items available for stealing are numerous, the methods of stealing are equally numerous, and the value of items stolen can be considerable. While each hotel will have its own organizational chart setting forth the responsibilities and functions of each department, for the purpose of this discussion we will consider the following services under the housekeeping department:

1. Care of guest rooms.
2. Laundry and/or linen room.
3. Housemen.

Specific threats which may occur will include, among others:

1. Thefts from guest rooms by employees or by others with or without the assistance of employees.
2. Thefts of hotel property by employees, guests or others.

3. Thefts of hotel or guests' property from public spaces.

In the food and beverage departments, supervision can be almost constant because the employees are physically confined by their working areas. For example, a cook is confined to the kitchen, a bartender stays with his bar, a waiter is either in the kitchen or in the dining room and he is supervised in either location. In the housekeeping department, on the other hand, the demands of an employee's job may require him to be in various areas. This makes supervision more difficult and makes it difficult to determine at a glance if an employee is out of his proper working area. As we discuss the duties of the housekeeping department, this will become more apparent.

CARE OF GUEST ROOMS

The security of guest rooms was covered in Chapter 5; we will concentrate here on the activities of housekeeping employees in the guest rooms. Normally, the care and cleaning of rooms is entrusted to a maid who is assigned a given number of rooms. Naturally, this maid has unlimited access to each room in her section. She knows at all times what rooms are occupied and which are vacant. She can spend as much time in a guest room as she desires without creating suspicion, since she always has the excuse that she is performing her duties. There is usually ample time for the maid to search any room thoroughly and discover the location of valuables. She has the opportunity to steal them herself or to notify a confederate who can accomplish the theft at a later date or time. A dishonest maid with a pass key in her possession is a very serious security threat.

Key Control

Control of pass keys or master keys is vital to a security program. Maids and others should be required to sign for their keys at the start of their shift. Keys should be checked in at the conclusion of the working day. Each employee entrusted with a key should be required to sign a contract or agreement that a charge (of $10 or some other agreed amount) will be deducted from his pay in the event the assigned key is lost. This may help to make the employee "key conscious," but naturally it will not prevent the employee from making an impression of the key if future criminal activities are planned. This is a strong argument in favor of the new "keyless" systems where lock combinations can be changed at will very inexpensively, thereby eliminating the danger of keys being reproduced.

An example of a keyless locking system is the "card-reader" equipment referred to in Chapter 5. The system can be programmed so that the maid's card will open guest room doors only during certain hours, thereby reducing the security risk.

Purposes of Supervision

Every attempt should be made to check prior employment before hiring a maid. Once hired, the new maid should be subjected to close supervision. In large establishments, there are usually assistant housekeepers or inspectresses who periodically check on each maid. This check serves several purposes:

1. The inspectress checks on the quality of work being performed—whether the room is clean, bed made properly, necessary supplies made available.
2. Any special instructions can be passed on to the maid at this time.
3. Any problems the maid might be having can be discussed at this time, whether they concern her duties, the conditions of rooms, or the need for supplies.
4. At the same time, if the inspectress has been properly trained, she can perform a security service by checking the maid's utility closet, her cart and working habits.

Unfortunately, the hotel will probably not know whether a maid is a thief until a theft takes place. Even then the hotel must not be too quick to accuse the maid. The theft might have been committed by someone else or may turn out to be only a misplaced item. Certainly, any reported loss warrants an investigation. Should a number of losses involve the same maid, suspicion would certainly be directed to that person.

Security-Conscious Maids

Maids should be required to leave the door open when they are working in a room. This not only permits anyone looking for the maid to find her, but also allows the maid to see who might be moving about in the halls. A good maid is security-conscious, but her security value is limited if she is out of sight. One word of caution, however, is in order regarding the open bathroom door. When the maid is cleaning and servicing the bathroom, she should be certain that the room door is then closed, as she may be running water and would be unable to hear anyone entering the room to commit a theft. At no time should a guest room door be left open if the room is unattended.

There is also a responsibility on the part of maids, as well as others acting as agents for the hotel owner, to forewarn guests of possible dangers and in this way to minimize possible injuries. This responsibility and duty was brought forcibly to the attention of the industry in the Howard Johnson's Hotel case in New Orleans. A maid was informed of the presence of an armed man on the property and was advised to warn the maid on another floor. The maid failed to pass this information on to her fellow employee, even though she did go to the floor as directed and engaged the maid working there in conversation for almost five minutes before the gunman appeared. No effort was made to warn the guests to remain in their rooms until the situation could be brought under control. In short, nothing was done to assist the guests or to inform them of possible danger. Instruction must be provided to employees in what is expected of them in such situations, as well as in assisting during evacuations in fire or other emergency conditions.

In order to be fully security-conscious, the maid must be properly instructed. There should be nothing done on her floor or in her section that she does not know about. Anyone or anything that is suspicious should be reported immediately. In many instances maids have discovered and reported fires, sneak-thieves and missing property. In addition, many have warned management of "skippers" or potential room thieves. While some maids might be thieves, the great majority are honest, hard-working, and more than willing to perform their duties for the good of the hotel.

Collusion and Sneak Thieves

Not all stealing from guest rooms is done by maids. The maid may be a party to the theft by advising a confederate of which rooms to "hit" and may even provide the key to the room. The theft may occur without the maid's knowledge. One thing is certain, however—if the theft involves the property of a guest, the maid will be the first to be blamed. This is a fact that should be made very clear to a new maid so that she will realize the need to be alert for her own protection.

The "sneak thief" is usually a professional, but more and more amateurs are getting into the act. We have already discussed the need for good locks, key control, and reporting of suspicious persons. Aside from these steps there is little we can do to prevent this type of theft.

Preventing Theft by Guests

Another potential thief is the occupant of the room himself. This is a particularly dangerous type of theft in motels. Because many motel units have private entrances to bedrooms, the guests can come and go as they please unnoticed. Many a television set, along with blankets, linens, lamps and pictures, has been removed in the dark of night and loaded into a waiting car.

Mention has already been made in Chapter 5 of the use of engraving tools to mark hotel property, tamper-proof hardware to make removal more difficult, alarm sensors to signal the tampering with or removal of equipment, fixtures or items from a guest room. These theft-deterrent methods must be given serious consideration if management desires to limit the number of thefts from guest rooms. If electronic systems are to be utilized, it is much less costly to design them into the building to be installed at the time of construction rather than adding them at a later time. Even if the system itself is not to be installed immediately, having the necessary wiring present for future use can be a substantial savings.

While some hotel registration cards include a space for entering the license number of the guest's automobile, often this space is left blank or the number filled in is not checked by the registration clerk. In some areas, such as parts of Canada, a guest cannot legally be forced to disclose his license number. However, if the space is provided for it on the registration blank, he may fill it in without hesitation. If he fails to do so, it is an easy matter for the clerk to secure the license plate number on his own after the guest is settled.

Certainly if a man plans to "strip" a room, he is not going to give his correct name or address, nor is he going to put down his correct license number. A great number of thefts, therefore, could be avoided if the guest were asked to provide some form of identification upon registration. If management does not want to embarrass the guest, at least a check should be made of the license number entered on the registration card to be certain that it agrees with the plate appearing on the vehicle. Then if a theft does occur, the police can be notified and the license checked, the owner identified and contacted. Such action on the part of the motel manager will help to curtail thefts by guests.

In the hotel, on the other hand, it is a bit more difficult for the guest to walk out to his car with a television set, although linens and other items that can be hidden in a suitcase may be removed. This is another opportunity for the maid to be of great assistance. An inspection should be made of the room as soon as it is vacated if at all possible. In addition, the maid's observations of the amount of luggage and clothing in a guest's room might be a tip-off of planned theft. Such observations should be reported by the maid to the proper authorities—the inspectress or the security department.

Employee Theft of Hotel Property

The guest may not be the only one desiring to steal linens. The maid herself may not be interested in the contents of a guest's room, but she may find hotel property very desirable. In the course of her normal duties, the maid is supplied with linens, blankets, pillows, towels, cleaning supplies, stationery and writing instruments, ash trays, matches and other items. It is true that some of these items are placed in the guest room with the hope the guest will take them as souvenirs. The fact to remember, however, is that these items are for the convenience of the guest who is spending money in the hotel, and not for the employee.

The presence of any of these items in the maid's utility room would not raise suspicion since they belong there. However, the inspectress or housekeeper should watch requisitions for replenishment of supplies to be certain excessive amounts or too frequent orders are not being made. Again, the installation of a package pass or package inspection system will prevent the removal of large items from the hotel. Maids should also be advised to keep their utility closets locked when unattended to prevent others from stealing the same items.

Other Persons Entering Rooms

In addition to the maids, there are other employees who will be entering the guest room, although not as frequently. In large hotels there may be window washers, vacuum men who are responsible for heavy cleaning, maintenance personnel and people from the drapery department. On occasion the valet, bootblack and laundry clerk may also enter the room. It can be seen that a number of people have legitimate reasons for entering a guest room.

A record should be kept in each department indicating what employees entered what rooms during a given day. For example, the laundry department will have a record of all rooms to which personal laundry was delivered. The vacuum men will have a list of rooms they are responsible for cleaning on a given day; this record should be retained in the housekeeper's office. In the event a theft does take place, the security officer can check with each department and compile a list of all who were known to have entered that particular room. While this system may not solve a particular crime, it may help to establish a pattern if it is discovered that in each case where a theft has occurred, a certain person has been in the room that day.

When one considers all the persons who have legitimate access to the guest room, it is obvious that the room is not as secure as might be expected. Management and the security officer must be aware of this and remain on guard constantly to maintain the greatest possible security.

LAUNDRY AND LINEN ROOM

Various problems can arise which point out the need for proper supervision in the handling of guest laundry. Personal items may be lost or delivered to the wrong room. The security officer is not directly involved, although he may be called upon to assist in locating lost or misplaced items.

The big danger to the hotel rests in the handling of its own laundry—bed linens, dining room linens, towels and uniforms. As is the case with other items, there is a need to safeguard these items properly when not in use, issue them only to the proper persons, ensure they are used for proper purposes, and prevent their theft. Whether these linen items are laundered in the hotel or by an outside contractor, the problem remains the same: there must be a supply on hand and this supply is subject to theft and misuse. Let us assume for the sake of this discussion that the hotel supplies its own linens rather than leasing them.

Receipt and Storage of Linen

Normally, when new stocks of linens are purchased, they are delivered to the linen room where they are unpacked and checked. Such items are usually delivered in large cases weighing several hundred pounds, almost impossible to steal because of their size. Once the large shipping case is opened, however, the contents are normally in smaller, individually wrapped packages of one dozen or more items per package. Such a package can be stolen much more easily.

It is vital that, when these cases are being unpacked, care be taken to make an accurate count of goods received and to ensure that none disappear in the process of unpacking. The supplies should be stored in a secure location until required for use.

Identifying Marks

In large hotels, sheets are marked with the hotel's name or decal, and towels and table linen have the name or initials of the hotel woven into the fabric. This is a great aid in identifying these goods when question of ownership arises. Where the hotel's name is not included on the items, some identifying mark should be made before they are placed in use.

Linen Cycle

Normally, the linen room issues all linen supplies, placing new supplies in use as the need develops. The linens go from the linen room to the individual maids or to the dining rooms, are used, returned as soiled linen, are laundered and then returned again to the linen room where they are inspected, repaired if necessary, and placed in service once again.

At any point in this cycle, the linen may be lost or stolen. Accurate records kept in the linen department will indicate the amount of loss, but they will not reveal how or where the loss is taking place. Yearly, a physical inventory should be taken of linen stocks. At that time, by taking the starting inventory, adding the purchases made during the year, deducting the number of items removed from service due to unfit condition, and comparing this figure with the actual count at the end of the year, the losses will be determined. Part of this loss will be due to theft and a portion will be due to careless losses on the part of employees.

Carelessness in Linen Handling

Carelessness is the easier of the two forms of loss to control. Linens may be thrown into the trash by mistake or intentionally. If some care is taken in trash removal, such linens can be salvaged. Loss also takes place when linens are used for purposes other than that intended and have to be removed from service due to condition. Examples would be a waiter using a napkin to shine his shoes or to wipe up spills on the floor; a cook using a napkin to wipe down his working area; a painter using a sheet as a drop cloth. Through normal attrition, there will be a supply of old sheets or other linen that can be provided by the linen room upon request. Proper materials should be available so there is no excuse for using expensive linens for these other needs.

Theft of Linen

Linens may be stolen by the employee or the guest. Almost every employee in the back of the house has access to some form of linen. If proper records are maintained, comparisons can be made of amounts requisitioned and volume of business experienced. To put it in the simplest terms, if a dining room orders 20 dozen napkins per day, but the records indicate they are only serving 150 meals per day and the excess stock is not in their supply closet, a question should certainly be raised as to where the extra napkins are located.

The amount of clean linen issued each day should have a direct relationship to the amount of soiled linen returned for laundering. If a significant difference occurs, it then becomes a question of where the difference is occurring, and the security officer must investigate the various possibilities. Linen is an expensive item and one that management would be wise to keep under close check. The assistance of all department heads and supervisors is vital if this matter is to be controlled.

HOUSEMEN

This job classification as we use it is all-inclusive. In many hotels the duties may be broken down into specific jobs and job titles, including vacuum men, cleaners, display and banquetmen, and others. In all but the largest hotels, a houseman may be required to perform any or all of these services, as well as others. We have already discussed the potential security threat posed when housemen enter guest rooms for any purpose. Another area of potential danger occurs when housemen are used to set up convention displays or to break down banquet or meeting rooms. Let us consider first the problem of setting up convention displays.

Convention Display Materials

When a convention including displays is scheduled, materials are normally shipped to the hotel ahead of time to be held pending the arrival of the sales representatives. Naturally, the hotel must accept these advance shipments. Immediately upon receipt, the hotel has an obligation to protect the material until it is called for by the addressee. Consequently, secure areas must be provided for the storage of these items and they must be afforded a high degree of security.

Once the time has come to erect the display, the materials are normally delivered to the display area by a houseman. The material is unpacked, with or without the assistance of the houseman, and the empty packing cases are removed and stored until the close of the show. The removal of the empty packing cases provides an excellent opportunity for stealing items. The sales representative or person in charge of erecting the display should be alert and should account for all his merchandise before the empty cases are removed. It takes only a fraction of a second to slip some item into an empty packing case and walk away. It is highly advisable that a guard be placed at the entrance to the display hall and that all material coming in or going out may be required to pass this guard. It will then be his responsibility to inspect every empty carton, box, or other container leaving the hall. This procedure may be time-consuming, but if experience has shown a history of thefts under these circumstances, this is one effective preventive measure that can be taken.

The degree of security needed will depend a great deal, of course, on the type of merchandise being displayed. Large, heavy equipment, for example, will not require the same degree of security against theft as smaller, more desirable items. The possibility of malicious damage to large items, however, must also be recognized.

When an exhibition is located within the hotel, arrangements should be made with the sponsors to provide proper security not only during the time the display area is open, but also during the hours when no one is in attendance. Just who is going to be responsible for maintaining the security required should be agreed upon in advance and stated in a written formal agreement. If the hotel is asked to undertake this job, additional guards will probably have to be provided for an around-the-clock security detail. Naturally, the convention sponsors will be required to reimburse the hotel for the expense of the guards. If the sponsors contract on their own for a guard service, the hotel's liability is somewhat reduced.

At the conclusion of an exhibit, the materials must be repacked and held for shipment to the next point of destination. The hotel normally assumes the responsibility of holding the material and seeing that it is picked up by the proper shipper. Measures must be taken to prevent losses while the display material is in the care and custody of the hotel.

Meetings and Banquets

Housekeeping department personnel may also become in-volved in the breaking down, clearing or servicing of a room following a meeting or banquet. Quite often items of clothing or other personal belongings are left behind by the departing guests. Ladies may leave sweaters or fur stoles, gloves and pocketbooks. Earrings may be dropped unnoticed. Men may leave briefcases, eyeglasses, and any number of other items of varying value which should be protected and secured for the owners. Whenever possible, it is well for a security officer to check a room carefully following any function and take custody of any items found. Where this is impractical, the houseman in charge should be instructed to perform this service, turning over anything found to the proper authority.

Chapter 11

Maintenance, Parking and Other Service Departments

The number of departments in a hotel will vary from one establishment to another; the employees may range in number from 2 or 3 to 2,000; the number of rooms may vary from 1 to 1,000. As long as the establishment deals with the public, provides services and accommodations, and as long as it has employees, it has a need for security. The problems, risks and hazards may differ, but it is necessary for management or the owner to determine what his specific problems are and to take steps necessary to protect not only his investment but also the lives and property of those he serves.

In this and the following chapters we will touch on some of the departments normally associated with a hotel operation and discuss some of the more common hazards that these departments face. It would be impossible to set forth all possible hazards, and it would serve no real purpose because of the varying economic, social and legal circumstances faced by each property. We can only hope to give some insight into what might occur, what can be done to prevent such occurrences, and what the individual hotel security officer should be concerned with.

MAINTENANCE AND ENGINEERING DEPARTMENTS

Most hotels and motels have a person or persons delegated responsibility for minor repairs and maintenance. Larger establishments will have a staff including painters, plasterers, carpenters,

139

plumbers, electricians, firemen, stationary engineers, air conditioning and refrigeration engineers, and others. All of these professional men require tools and supplies to practice their trades, and
it is obviously more economical to purchase these supplies in
quantity rather than on an "as needed" basis. With thousands of
light bulbs in a hotel, for example, it would be impractical to buy
light bulbs by the dozen on a day-to-day basis. The same holds
true for other supplies.

The stock of supplies therefore must be protected, issued
only as needed and accounted for. Just as a waiter may think
nothing of "snitching" a piece of bacon, so a maintenance
employee may think nothing of stealing a package of fuses for use
at home. Multiply this small item by 365 days a year or by any
number of individual thefts, and the resulting losses can amount to
a great deal of money. Once again, loss prevention becomes a
matter of control within the department and close supervision on
the part of the department head.

Records Required

Adequate records must be kept and referred to frequently. In
larger establishments, each maintenance man may be required to
turn in a work sheet for each day's work, showing what was
accomplished and the materials used on that day. This provides a
time and material record for the department to justify its
expenses. If continual issues of a given item are made to a
mechanic, but there are no work sheets to support the use of such
items and they are not located in his working stock, a question is
automatically raised as to where the material disappeared to and
what it was used for.

Most of the items used in the maintenance department can
also be used in the average home and are therefore very susceptible
to theft. Unfortunately, many of these items are small and can be
carried out easily by a man in his pants pocket. This is all the more
reason why accurate records must be kept of supplies issued and
materials used on a given job.

Mechanical Operations

Maintenance and engineering personnel also have a responsibility to maintain the mechanical operations of the hotel. Neglect

or poor workmanship on their part can cause breakdowns that can be disastrous. Routine servicing and maintenance is a must to prolong the life of any mechanical device. In this realm, a security officer and security patrols can be of great assistance. In the course of their routine patrols, they may discover matters that need attention. Prompt attention to a noisy motor or a squeaking wheel, a broken door-check or a sticking door may prevent a complete breakdown at a later date. All mechanical devices should be scheduled for periodic maintenance and service on a routine basis and this should be supervised by the department head. Security personnel should not hesitate to report apparent or potential troubles that come to their attention.

Secure Areas

The maintenance and engineering departments also have a responsibility to keep their own areas secure from unauthorized personnel. Stockrooms should not be left unattended. Areas where machinery is located should be properly secured. A perfect example of the lack of such security occurred recently in a group of hotels. A labor dispute was underway involving elevator service personnel and a leading elevator firm. In an act of terrorism or defiance, striking mechanics entered a number of hotels, went to the elevator penthouses and damaged the equipment, putting the elevators out of service. Had these persons been required to enter a service entrance and sign in, at least the hotel would have had the names of the intruders. Had the unattended and vital machine area been secured, the mechanics could not have entered without first obtaining a key to the area unless they were prepared to make forced entry, which would have compounded their crime.

The heart of a hotel is in its engineering area, and it is vital that security be maintained. The importance of protecting these areas should be realized by all concerned. Just because these areas are normally in the "bowels" of the hotel, they should not be overlooked or slighted when it comes to preventing theft or interruption of services.

PARKING FACILITIES

Parking has become one of the biggest problems faced by today's innkeeper. In the infancy of the hotel industry, the innkeeper was as much concerned with the care of his guest's horse as with the guest himself. The law placed an obligation upon the innkeeper to provide proper shelter for the horse and to render such care as was reasonable. The innkeeper in effect had two guests, one human and the other animal.

We have progressed from animal power to automotive power, and our problems have grown in complexity. The problem, in many respects, is governed by local regulations; each property should determine what is required in its own jurisdiction. Many localities require that a certain number of off-the-street parking spaces be provided in relation to the number of rooms available. Naturally, any hotel or motel must realize the need to provide parking areas, but how much should be provided, where it should be located, and how it will be operated will depend on a number of factors in addition to local ordinances. Considerations that will have to be made include:

1. The size of the hotel and the number of rooms.
2. The nature of the operation; for example, whether the hotel provides amenities such as food, beverage and entertainment which may be patronized by persons other than those to whom rooms have been allotted.
3. Financial considerations and availability of adjacent land.

The evaluation of these factors will depend entirely on local circumstances, but the space provided for parking should be as large as necessary consistent with financial considerations. It is not good for business if patrons must rely on meter street parking, or if cars must be parked some distance away. These two circumstances should be avoided whenever possible.

Parking lots should adjoin the premises if possible, but the hotel's main entrance must be kept open for loading and unloading. It is permissible for the hotel to erect signs prohibiting parking at the main entrance and directing traffic to the parking lot, provided those signs are placed on hotel property. If signs must be placed upon a public street or thoroughfare, permission of the municipality is required. The lot should provide easy access and sufficient room to maneuver. Where possible, parking spaces should be marked out to prevent odd angle parking that might use extra space and impede the normal flow of traffic.

The problems that can occur on a parking lot or in a garage are numerous. Among these problems are:

1. Damage to an automobile caused by a patron driving his own car.
2. Damage to an automobile caused by an employee or agent of the hotel.
3. Theft of an automobile.
4. Theft of the contents of an automobile.

Other considerations depend on the operation itself. Is the parking area limited to the use of hotel guests only or is it also offered to the general public? How will guest parking be handled? Will the guest be required to park his own car or will valet service be provided? If valet service is provided, what laws will be involved? For example, in Ontario, Canada, the Highway Traffic Act formerly required employees driving guest cars from the main entrance to the parking area to hold chauffeurs' licenses. Depending on the type of liability insurance applied for, certain requirements may be set forth relative to these "car jockeys" as well as other requirements for the security of the area.

While some hotels provide free parking for their guests, others may charge for this added service. If charges are made, the problem arises of accounting for money collected. Will the garage attendant collect the money, or will the charge be placed on the guest's bill and paid as part of his general account? It would be our recommendation that if charges are to be made for parking, these charges be placed directly on the guest's account, thereby eliminating the handling of any cash between the guest and the garage attendant.

Garage Security

Garages, whether private or available to the public as well as to hotel patrons, provide another location where potential muggers, rapists, thieves and others can wait in hiding to attack their prey. This is especially true where the operation is a "park-it-yourself" system. The valet type service is far more acceptable from a security standpoint, since only authorized persons are permitted beyond the entrance. However, care must be taken that no other means of access—such as low fences, windows, etc.—are available to the potential thief.

Where a parking area is located directly beneath a hotel, motel or any tenant-occupied building, it is strongly recommended that access to that building not be permitted directly from the parking level through unsupervised means of access; rather, parkers should be required to pass first through a supervised entrance. Referring again to the Howard Johnson's situation, the hotel was designed with seven floors or levels of parking beneath ten floors of sleeping accommodations. The garage area was open to the public as well as to guests of the hotel and was a park-it-yourself system. From the various levels of the garage, anyone could enter an elevator serving the entire structure and thereby go to any floor of the hotel undetected.

The purpose of such a system was the convenience of the guests, who could park their cars and go directly to their accommodations. It is obvious that persons other than guests, who had no right to be in the hotel, could also gain entrance in the same manner. Although the gunman did not use this means of entry to the hotel, he could very well have done so without detection. In instances such as this a choice must be made between convenience and safety. Safety should be the first consideration of management.

Parking Lot Security

While insurance can be secured to limit liability for the theft of cars or their contents, it is rather embarrassing for an innkeeper to inform a guest that his car has been stolen or broken into while the innkeeper had the vehicle in his custody. The innkeeper should take whatever steps he can to prevent such incidents. Naturally, the ideal situation would be to have an enclosed garage with one exit, manned at all times by an attendant with some system of claim checks in use. Obviously, the ideal facilities are not always feasible, and management is forced to operate with what is available. Steps that might be considered relative to parking lot security include:

1. Enclosure of the entire area with fencing of sufficient height to discourage trespassers.
2. Sufficient lighting at night to prevent persons from hiding or operating under cover of darkness.

3. Use of closed circuit television scanning the parking areas, monitored by an attendant at all times.
4. The posting of proper notices, where permitted by law or by conditions set forth in the insurance program, relative to the liability assumed by management.

What is done and how it is done will depend almost entirely on the advice of legal counsel and the requirements of the insurance in effect. This matter should be thoroughly discussed and such steps as are appropriate should be instituted and strictly enforced.

In congested areas, parking at the main entrance of a hotel can create a serious problem. Where the main entrance is on a public street, the parking regulations will be the responsibility of the municipal police or parking authority. However, if the entrance is on hotel property, suitable warning signs should be erected and drivers should be asked to obey such "no parking" restrictions. Failure to comply with these regulations is cause for management to have the offending automobile towed away at the owner's expense.

Before such action is declared policy, however, legal advice should be secured to determine the hotel's liability should the car be damaged in the act of towing or at the place to which it is towed. Naturally, such an action on the part of management will not create good public relations, and before such drastic action is taken, every attempt should be made to have the owner comply with the regulations pertaining to parking.

Reporting Damage

Along the lines of good public relations, it should be the policy of the hotel that, if and when an accident does occur and a guest's car is damaged by a hotel employee or by another party, the car's owner should be notified as soon as possible rather than waiting until the owner calls for the car prior to departure. If the damage is serious, there may be time to make minor repairs if not completely repairing the car. The adjuster for the hotel's insurance carrier may witness the damage and perhaps arrive at a settlement, thereby eliminating much correspondence concerning the matter.

Management should also make a point of carefully investigating every claim for damages to an automobile, since many persons will attempt to blame the hotel for damages that were present when the car arrived. A good degree of tact and firmness is necessary in handling such claims. If the hotel does not wish to become fully involved, the matter can be referred to the insurance carrier.

At best, the parking situation is a necessary evil to management. Since it is a service that must be provided, however, it is one that hotel management must be prepared to handle.

Special Problems of Motel Parking Lots

The problems of parking lot security in a small establishment are to a great extent dependent on the physical layout of the property. The steps that must be taken to provide security likewise will depend on these conditions. The ideal situation would require that parking be within an internal courtyard as opposed to parking on the perimeter of the property. In this manner, coming and going of guests could be controlled through one entry or exit way which could be located within vision of the business office.

Lighting is important regardless of parking lot location to deter muggers and car thieves from lurking in the darkness and shadows. Care must be taken to focus lights in such a manner that the parking area is illuminated without causing glare to shine into guest rooms.

The use of closed circuit television to monitor parking areas is within the financial ability of some motel operators. The camera coverage can be monitored by the office personnel. Again, the feasibility of such equipment will depend on the actual physical layout of the area to be covered.

Motel personnel should make a periodic check of the parking area to ensure that guests have locked their vehicles with the windows closed. Clear and complete statements limiting the liability of the motel operator relative to guests' vehicles and the contents thereof should be posted conspicuously. When the guest drives his car up to the unit he has rented and parks in the space provided, his vehicle is not part of the motel manager's responsibility. It is suggested that management, after obtaining legal advice, inform guests in writing when they register that the motel will not be responsible for cars or contents, and that they are left on the premises entirely at their owners' risk.

OTHER SERVICE DEPARTMENTS

Bellmen

Bellmen, doormen and checkroom attendants also become involved in details where security may play an important part. Bellmen may be called to guest rooms for a number of reasons and therefore have an opportunity to commit thefts. In addition, their appearance at any location throughout the hotel would not arouse suspicion, as the nature of their duties requires them to cover almost the entire hotel area. These men not only room a guest upon initial arrival but perform a number of service functions at the request of the guest during his stay.

A bellman's call sheet should be maintained with the bell captain recording every request for a bellman, the individual bellman handling the call, the room to which he responded, the nature of the call, the time "out" and the time returned. If there is a question as to who did what and when, there will be a record available.

Packages are often received for guests. In some hotels it has been the practice not to allow deliverymen to make deliveries directly to a guest room, but to require the package to be delivered to the front desk or the bellman's desk for handling. This is a good practice since it prevents unknown persons from entering the sleeping floors. At this point, some hotels make a mistake and permit the bellman to deliver the package to the guest room. If the guest is not in his room, the bellman enters the room and deposits the package.

This practice should and can be avoided. The guest room should be called by telephone and, if the guest is in, the package may be delivered. If the guest is not in his room, a package notice may be placed on his door asking him to contact the desk or the bellman upon his return, or a message may be left with the telephone operator if automatic message signaling devices are provided in each guest room.

Bellmen are often requested to check luggage or packages for guests who have vacated their rooms but are not yet ready to depart from the hotel, or who do not wish to carry the item with them for a period of time. Such a service should be handled in the same manner as a checkroom attendant would check an overcoat or a hat. The guest must be given a claim check. Once a claim check is given, the hotel becomes responsible for the safekeeping of the items checked. Therefore, the check area should not be left unattended, and no items should be handed out without a claim stub to identify the articles.

Once an item is turned over to the innkeeper or any of his agents or employees for safekeeping, the item is physically transferred from the guest or patron directly to the employee, and a claim check or receipt is exchanged, the hotel becomes solely liable in most cases. Therefore, bellmen and checkroom attendants must be instructed carefully in their responsibilities and must never leave the items in their charge unattended.

Doormen

The duties of the doorman in keeping obviously undesirable persons from entering the hotel were discussed in Chapter 4. There is an additional responsibility on the part of the doorman that warrants comment. Often the doorman assists in the loading of an automobile with the luggage of a guest. Close attention must be paid to placing the proper luggage in the proper car. The doorman should make a point of checking closely with the owner as to the identification of his luggage and the proper number of pieces to avoid the embarrassment and confusion created when a piece of luggage is placed in the wrong car and that car takes off for points unknown. Such a loss can create very hard feelings and can be an expensive error for the hotel.

Doormen must also be instructed in the requirements for safety in their duties. It might seem like a small matter, but the entrance of a hotel is an area where a great number of accidents occur. Persons may be struck by automobiles, automobiles themselves may be involved in accidents, passengers may be injured by a door closing on their fingers, etc. In most cases where such accidents do occur, the hotel will be held liable; it will be claimed that an attendant was present and it was his duty to maintain order and control the situation so that accidents could not take place. There have been many cases where a doorman has shut a car door on a person's fingers, and in each instance it has been stated that the doorman was not devoting the proper amount of attention to his duties and was therefore liable.

Lost and Found Department

Lost-and-found is usually not a department within itself but rather a service under the control and responsibility of another department. Its services and functions, however, are important to management.

There should be an understanding between management and employee, established at the time of hiring, that any item "found" within the hotel becomes the property of the hotel and must be turned over to the proper authority. The old slogan of "finders keepers, losers weepers" cannot apply. The hotel may establish the regulation that any found item turned in to the hotel, if not claimed by the rightful owner within a specific time, may be claimed by the finder. This would be a fair approach and one that management may consider as a matter of policy.

Every item found by an employee on the premises, regardless of its worth, should be turned over to a specific person or office. The item should be properly tagged and an entry should be made in an official record indicating:

1. A description of the "found" article,
2. Where it was found,
3. When it was found,
4. The name of the person who found the article.

The item should then be stored in a safe place.

It is surprising to the uninformed how many items are lost or forgotten by guests. Articles of clothing, razor cords, jewelry, books, false teeth, important papers and many other items are often left in hotel rooms. Often the guest will contact the hotel after his departure to inquire if such items have been found and request they be forwarded to him. In other cases, the owner may not realize where his loss took place or have no desire to regain his possessions. Whether or not the hotel wishes to attempt to locate the owner will be a matter of policy, but the fact remains that these items must be properly recorded and held for a period of time, pending a claim for recovery.

Hotel Switchboard

While there is normally little chance for fraud or theft in connection with the telephone department, the services provided by this department can be vital to the security officer. Emergency messages are normally transmitted by telephone and the proper handling of these messages can determine the outcome of an incident.

While we realize that a reliable operator does not "listen in" on conversations, there are times when such action may be called for and it will be necessary for management to bend the regulations slightly. Often, background noises and conversations overheard by an operator in the normal course of her duties can be a "tip-off" that something may be out of order or a problem may be in the making. If the security officer is notified, preventive or protective measures can be taken in time to prevent more serious problems. Any unusual occurrence naturally should be brought to the attention of the security department immediately. For example, if a call from a guest room is not completed and no response is received by the operator although the telephone has not been returned to the cradle, the possibility that the caller has been taken ill or is in some type of trouble must be considered and investigated immediately. (The role of the telephone operator in response to a bomb threat call is discussed in Chapter 16.)

The records of the telephone department are vital in an investigation, so it is important that these records be maintained properly. Communications in any security system are vital, and it goes without saying that they must be kept in good order, whether the system consists of the common telephone or some sophisticated transmitting and receiving device.

Chapter 12

Administrative Offices

In discussing the security that must be maintained for administrative offices, we will be referring to the following services, whether each is confined to a private office space or several are grouped together. The list may not be complete for a particular hotel, but the reader will be able to apply the principles to whatever services exist.

1. Personnel
2. Accounting
3. Paymaster
4. Sales (including sub-departments such as Catering, Banquet, Convention Service, etc.)
5. Credit
6. Security
7. Purchasing
8. Executive

OFFICE THEFTS

Common Targets

Since the security of money will be discussed in Chapter 13, we will not concern ourselves here with this phase of the problem. Other than cash, what contents of these offices would be susceptible to theft? Among the possibilities are:

151

1. Office machines (typewriters, adding machines, dictating machines, etc.)
2. Office supplies
3. Records of every type (financial, payroll, tax, personnel, etc.)
4. Financial instruments (checks and checkwriting machines).

While the uninformed might feel that the only really valuable thing listed above would be the office machines, it is certain that no businessman desires his financial statements—or, for that matter, any of his business records—to be made public. Loss of such records for any reason would create a tremendous accounting problem. Many an innkeeper would gladly pay for a list of his competition's past, present and potential convention contacts. Competition is the name of the game for many hotels, and many times there are no rules that apply to business ethics between properties. Blank checks in the hands of the wrong person could also cause havoc.

Office supplies may not seem like a big issue, but small amounts of such things taken on a routine basis can add up to a considerable amount of money. A few packages of paper here, a few dozen pencils there, some carbon paper or typewriter ribbons now and then, and many a schoolchild can be outfitted for the year. Stealing is stealing no matter what is involved; that is what the security officer is out to prevent.

Protection Recommendations

Since various hotels will differ in their physical arrangement, it would be difficult to make recommendations that would fit each situation. We can only offer certain suggestions that may be considered to maintain maximum security.

1. Fire-resistive files, cabinets and safes must be provided as needed for storage of those records and papers considered vital to the operation of the hotel. Such files and cabinets must be provided with satisfactory locking devices. They should be kept locked at all times when not in use.

Those day-to-day working papers vital to the hotel's operation or highly confidential in nature should be stored in a file cabinet with a dial lock. This type of mechanism offers additional security over a key-locked file cabinet. The combination should be changed on at least a six-month interval, or whenever the combination has been compromised, or upon termination of any employee with access to the file.

2. Vital or confidential papers should not be stored in a desk overnight but should be returned to the proper file, cabinet or safe.

3. At the end of the working day, desk tops should be cleared of all material and desks should be locked. In this manner casual passers-by cannot take or read what is lying on a desk. While a desk lock is normally not very strong, it provides at least some deterrent.

4. Excess office supplies should be kept in a locked closet or supply cabinet and issued by one person only.

5. Offices should be so designed that unauthorized persons can gain admittance only at the discretion of the occupant of that office.

6. Offices should never be left unlocked if unattended.

7. Windows in offices should be provided with some protection against illegal entry.

8. Consideration should be given to alarm systems, sensors, CCTV, or whatever device is felt necessary to protect the most valuable records. Microfilming of tax records, pay records and possibly other valuable papers, with the microfilm stored in a bank depository or some other location, may warrant consideration.

9. Janitorial services should be conducted under supervision or only by thoroughly trusted persons. Certainly a new employee should not be permitted to perform these services unescorted.

10. Financial work sheets, statements, or any personal or classified information to be destroyed, should be run through a shredding machine. This includes carbon paper used to make copies of such reports or statements. (There is nothing worse than having financial statements lying in the trash house or blowing around

the streets after having fallen from a trash truck.)

11. Keys to files, cabinets, etc., must be accounted for at all times and issued only to those persons who have a need to gain admittance to such areas.

12. Information pertaining to any records should be given only to authorized persons. If there is any doubt about a person's authorization to have access to records, the department supervisor should be contacted. The position of department head does not justify unlimited access to all information. Management should establish a policy as to who is entitled to payroll, personnel or financial information.

13. Records should not be permitted to leave any office unless prior authority from management is received, and then only after a signed receipt is obtained for the material being removed. No one should be allowed to take home records or other proprietary information without written consent of the innkeeper.

14. Confidential information of any kind concerning the hotel operation should not be discussed with employees from other offices or departments in public places—such as employee cafeteria, rest rooms, etc. Employees should be warned to respect the confidential nature of this information when in public or in the privacy of their homes. Hotel business should remain in the hotel.

15. All employees should be advised at the time of hiring that hotel records do not become the personal property of employees. Information pertaining to hotel operations acquired by an employee while working for the hotel becomes the property of the hotel and cannot be retained by the employee in the event of termination. (This should be made part of the written employment contract to be signed at the time of initial hiring. Legal advice should be secured in this matter.)

16. If it is deemed necessary or desirable, based on previous experience, consideration should be given to securing office machines to desk or table tops to prevent their theft. If the office is made secure and the other controls mentioned have been placed in effect, this action may not be necessary. Securing of machines in this manner

does create a bit of a problem at times, as they cannot be transferred from desk to desk or shared in an office.

Obviously there are other measures that can be taken; each situation must be judged on its own. Any attempt to compromise the security of these offices or any possible security leak should be brought to the attention of the supervisor immediately.

The security officer is concerned only with the physical security of these spaces and the persons working within the areas. The duties performed are controlled and supervised by the appropriate department head. It is his responsibility to ensure that fraud and deception do not take place. If suspicions are raised, the security department may be asked to assist in an investigation. Any person dealing with money or finances should be bonded for the protection of the hotel.

PERSONNEL-SECURITY COOPERATION

The personnel department is one area where there should be close cooperation with the security officer. If a hotel is not large enough to maintain a separate personnel department and each department head is allowed to hire his or her own employees, the problem is more difficult but not insurmountable. Ideally, every applicant for a position in the hotel should be interviewed, a complete history of employment secured, references listed, a physical examination given, and possibly some psychological testing conducted. If the right person is placed in the right job, the chances of error, turnover and inefficiency can be greatly reduced. Unfortunately, the opportunity for being one hundred percent selective is very limited. In some areas of the world, hotels are ready and willing to employ any applicant in order to fill needs. Therefore, in our comments, we can only recommend certain policies that would be of great assistance, if and when they can be adopted.

Hiring Policies

Before any person is hired, certain policies should be set forth by management. Many of the decisions that were formerly permitted management have been removed by legislation. For example, there can no longer be any discrimination because of sex, race or color. The minimum working age is established by law, as are hours of employment and many other aspects of working conditions. In many parts of the world today, there are programs to promote hiring of certain groups of people—veterans, former drug addicts, former convicts, handicapped persons, for example. Management will have to decide on the extent to which they wish to participate in such programs. While a man's past history is not supposed to affect his chances for respectable employment, we must be realistic in our approach. If we have a man who has just served time for a serious theft, we cannot in good conscience place him in a position of trust where he may handle money or other valuables. We may be willing to give him a less responsible job where he will have the opportunity to prove himself. If he performs in a satisfactory manner, we can consider promotions at a later date.

Checking References

Wherever possible, references and past employers should be contacted to ascertain the reliability, working habits, and ability of a prospective employee. Wherever possible, references and prior employment records should be checked by telephone or by a personal visit rather than by mail. Quite often a former employer is willing to make verbal comments that he would hesitate to reduce to writing.

As much of the information on the employment application as possible should be verified. If it is found that the applicant has lied, this should be reason enough to deny employment. One simple telephone call to a former employer might save many heartaches and problems later. Along these lines, there is a plea that is made by every sincere and dedicated personnel director; namely that, when information is required from a former employer concerning an applicant, the truth and the whole truth should be revealed. We are not interested in rumors or personal preferences but merely the facts in the matter. It is permissible to state that an employee was discharged due to certain suspicions or that he was discharged when actually caught in a theft. It is then the responsibility of the new personnel director to make a decision whether his establishment desires to take a chance on the applicant.

Character references should not carry too much weight unless the person listed is well known personally or by reputation or can be checked on easily. It is easy for an applicant to list friends or relatives as character references, and these persons may give false information. A prominent or important name may be given with the thought in mind that the personnel director will be impressed with the name alone and will never check further. If such a name is used on the application, it should be the first reference checked.

Confidentiality of Personnel Records

The material assembled by the personnel department in an employee's personal file is strictly confidential information. Indiscriminate publication of uncomplimentary or damaging information could result in a civil suit on the part of the injured party. There are a few people who should be aware of a possible problem if an employee with a questionable background is employed: the security officer and the department head. It should be made very clear, however, that the information is confidential and should be treated as such.

While responsible for the security of a large hotel, one of the authors had as employees two paroled murderers, several reformed drug addicts, and several men who had been convicted of fraud, illegal conversion, bad check passing and assorted other crimes. The history of these men was known only to the personnel director, the manager and the director of security. To this day, it is doubtful that any other employee in the hotel knew who or what these men had been in the past.

Many social reformers would fight to protect the rights of the individual with regard to his past history and would state that an employer has no right to inquire into a man's past. In fact, in some areas laws requiring those with criminal records to register with the police when moving into a new location have been declared unconstitutional. It is the opinion of others, however, that an employer has the right to know whom he is hiring, provided he uses that information in a confidential and fair manner. This is a problem for hotel management to solve in any way they see fit. But in any case where it is suspected that a problem might arise, the security officer should be advised in advance.

Chapter 13

Protecting Money and Valuables

Theft or loss of cash is one of the most serious security hazards confronting a hotel or motel. Money is the most attractive of all theft targets. For one thing, it can be used immediately by the thief and does not have to be "fenced." Further, the problem of identification arises. If a dollar bill is stolen and a person is apprehended with a dollar in his possession, is it the same dollar? This is almost impossible to prove in most circumstances, as people normally do not record the serial numbers of their bills and have no way of identifying one bill from another. These two factors alone make money a very attractive target.

CASH IN THE HOTEL

Operations Generate Cash

In the normal course of events, a hotel may generate large sums of cash in a given working day. This cash is accumulated in various ways such as:

1. Payment by guests for lodging, etc., at the check-out desk.
2. Bar receipts.
3. Restaurant receipts.
4. Revenue generated by shops or retail operations on the premises.

5. Vending machines.
6. Sums deposited with the hotel by guests for safekeeping.

The amount of cash handled may be reduced by the extensive use of credit cards and checks today, but many patrons still pay for purchases with cash. Not only must the hotel be concerned with cash collected from the patrons, but also with providing "banks"—supplies of cash for making change—to each cashier. In addition, if a particular hotel pays its employees in cash, there may be considerable amounts of money on hand to meet payday requirements.

Types of Threats to Cash

The threats to the money supplies in a hotel might be summarized as follows:

1. Robbery.
2. Theft by breaking and entering.
3. Theft by employees.
4. Theft by guests.

There are protective measures that may be implemented after considering local conditions and the particular hotel operation. Application of the following, with such modifications as may be required, will help to reduce the hazards.

Safes for Hotel Property

While no receptacle is completely theft-proof, many cannot be opened without considerable effort and expenditure of time. The hotel should provide a modern Underwriters' Laboratories approved safe for its own funds and other top security items. This safe should be restricted to items belonging to the hotel, as opposed to those facilities for the safekeeping of guests' property. Naturally, access to this safe should be very restrictive. The combination should be known to as few persons as possible and should be changed periodically, certainly upon the termination of any employee knowing it. The combination should be a series of numbers not related to any given person; for example, someone's birth date, Social Security number, or telephone number should not be used. This holds true for any safe within the hotel. While the security officer should not be a party to establishing the combination, he should ensure that the combinations are changed as needed and advise the type of combination to be used.

Setting Combinations

Some combination locks are difficult for the untrained person to change. Rather than attempt to make a change and risk snarling a lock, the following system has been used in many establishments with great success. A trained locksmith or a representative of the lock manufacturer prepares the lock for the insertion of a combination. The responsible party then places a combination on the lock and, without closing the door, locks the locking mechanism and attempts to open it with the new combination. In the event something has gone wrong, the door is open and the locksmith can remove the faulty combination. The responsible party can then apply a new set of numbers. In this manner, only the person who sets the combination knows the proper sequence of numbers.

Some companies prefer that the chief security officer set all combinations. This is feasible as long as the security officer is properly versed in the setting and removing of combinations. An argument in favor of this practice is that the security officer as well as the person responsible for the safe or file knows the combination; in the event one or the other is not available and the unit must be opened, the one present can provide the combination.

It is recommended that all combinations be recorded in some manner and placed in a bank vault or some other safe place for emergency use only. The most important points to remember, however, are that combinations should be changed at intervals or whenever required, and that as few people as possible should have knowledge of the combination.

Security personnel, as part of their routine rounds, should check closed safes and file cabinets equipped with any type of lock to ensure that the lock has been engaged and the door or drawer has not merely been closed without engaging the lock.

Cash Receptacles

√ All cash drawers, cash boxes, cash registers or other receptacles should be located so that an unauthorized person cannot reach in, over or around and help himself. They should all be provided with locks so that they may be secured if left unattended, even for a moment. Only the person having custody of the receptacle should have the key to that particular unit. In addition, only the person responsible should use a particular register or drawer. If two bartenders have access to the same cash register, it should be a register with two separate drawers and two separate banks.

Money should never be left in a receptacle overnight when the particular facility is closed for the night. In a restaurant, for example, all money should be removed from the register and turned in to the hotel cashier or placed in a night depository. Any bank retained for the following day's business should be deposited with the hotel cashier for safekeeping. When registers are emptied, the cash drawer should be left open so that it is obvious that no money is stored in it. This might save damage to an expensive register by someone attempting to break open a closed money drawer.

Where permanent registers or cash drawers are installed, consideration might be given to an alarm device in the drawer itself, like those often used by banks. "Bait money" is placed in a special compartment of the drawer; when it is removed, a silent alarm is activated automatically.

It is desirable whenever possible to use cashiers rather than having serving personnel handle or be responsible for cash. Consideration should also be given to having cashiers bonded.

Size of Banks

The amount of money supplied to any cashier for making change, or retained on hand by the Head Cashier to meet the needs of the hotel operations, should be no more than what is necessary to meet the demands of business. This is something that will have to be decided by the chief financial officer of the innkeeper. Normal accounting practices require a cashier to turn in all moneys over and above the amount of her bank, regardless of whether she has a shortage or an overage. It should also be a routine practice for the banks themselves to be checked by the head cashier at unannounced intervals. Cashiers have been known to use "bank" funds to cover shortages or for their own personal use. This must never be permitted.

It should be made abundantly clear to all persons entrusted with hotel money that, while they are to be held accountable for that money, they are not to risk their lives in the protection of same. If an armed holdup should occur, they are to offer no resistance that might endanger their lives or the lives of other persons in the immediate area. For this reason, management should review their insurance coverage carefully to ensure that the loss of any cash, whether from armed robbery, unlawful conversion or embezzlement by an employee, or by any other means, will be covered.

Vending Machine Receipts

Vending machines, requiring the payment of money to secure a product or entertainment, may be located on the hotel premises. These machines should be cleared of their cash on a routine basis—weekly or, if the business warrants, daily. The amount of money collected should be computed for each machine. The money and report should be turned in to the head cashier or some other authorized person. Vending machines should be located in a public place if possible to prevent undiscovered or unnoticed breaking and entering.

Transportation of Money

Money should be transported in some form of container, if for no other reason than to prevent its being dropped or lost. Cashiers should be able to transport their banks from the office to their place of operations without difficulty. At the end of a working shift, if their receipts are considerable, cashiers should be escorted from their place of operation to the main office. If excess money is collected during the course of a shift, arrangements should be made to have a portion of those receipts removed from the area and turned in to the head cashier.

There is scarcely a place on the earth today where it is wise to walk the streets with large sums of money. The bulk receipts from a hotel should be transported to the bank for deposit by an armored car service. If such is not reasonable or feasible, normally the local police are willing to arrange an escort to the bank. If neither of these options is suitable and money must be transported outside the hotel by an employee, on foot or in a vehicle, no set routine should be established as to time and route.

As the reader can quickly realize, the problem of securing cash and valuables is a difficult one that will require different approaches depending on various factors, including amounts involved, location, size, and physical layout of the hotel, incidence of crime in the area, and response time of local police. The security officer should recognize that money is a prime target, and he must therefore take the steps necessary in his particular situation to protect cash.

Motel Holdup Vulnerability

In a motel, a holdup is most likely to occur during the evening and nighttime hours when there are few witnesses available. Several precautions can be taken by the motel operator, including the following:

1. Remove any excess cash to a night depository or safe location, and maintain a very limited night bank.
2. Lock the office or lobby door after a given hour so that it can be opened only by the release of an electric lock by the night clerk after a caller has identified himself.
3. Install silent alarm systems connected to municipal police departments or central stations. The alarm can be triggered easily by the clerk in attendance. Such systems are valuable to large or small operators at any time of the day or night and are worth the expense.
4. Advertise a policy of accepting as little cash as possible, indicating to the potential thief that the rewards of a holdup would not outweigh the risks involved.
5. Do not rely solely on a sticker attached to the office window, advertising a security service, to ensure security. This practice may be a deterrent to a potential thief, but it is not complete protection.

6. Keeping a large dog, such as a German shepherd, on the premises may increase protection from attack.

SAFEKEEPING FOR GUESTS' PROPERTY

In addition to the hotel's safe, under the Innkeepers' Liability Law discussed earlier in this book provisions must be made for the safekeeping of moneys and other valuables belonging to the guests. Normally, such protection is in the form of safe deposit boxes like those used in banks. The hotel has a master key and each box has an individual key; both keys are required to open the box. Once items have been placed in the box, the guest retains the individual key. If extra keys are maintained for the individual boxes, they should be located in a bank deposit or at some location where they are under maximum security and available only to management.

Where such deposit boxes are not available, deposit envelopes are often provided with a claim tag attached. These envelopes may be stored together in one safe, with each depositor holding his own claim ticket. Upon presentation of this claim ticket and a signature, the corresponding envelope is returned to the ticket holder.

Because the law states that furs and other valuables must be protected by the hotel if requested by the guest, provisions must be made for the storage of these larger items which would not fit into an envelope or safe deposit box. Therefore a theft-resistant, fire-proof vault or cabinet of some type must be provided.

High Security Desirable

These safes, boxes and vaults must never be left unlocked and/or unattended. They deserve the utmost degree of security, and any steps deemed necessary to establish that security must be undertaken if economically feasible. While the hotel has a limited liability for items stolen from a safe deposit box, it would be far more satisfactory if the theft could be prevented in the first place.

A series of thefts took place in New York City a few years ago wherein a group of professional thieves entered a hotel, overpowered the employees and proceeded to open a number of safe deposit boxes containing the valuables of the guests. While their work took more than one hour and required drilling and other methods of breaking open the boxes, they went undetected and were able to escape without incident. Although this seems almost impossible, it happened not once but several times.

Extra Protection for Valuables

The following precautions should be considered for protecting valuables.

1. The use of commercial, silent alarm systems such as those used by banks, which can be triggered by employees without alerting the thief.
2. The use of alarm systems designed to detect any action such as moving, hammering, drilling or in any manner tampering with the safe.
3. The use of CCTV in connection with the opening of any safe or vault. This device can be installed to record on tape the presence of any person coming within the perimeter of the protected area. This would at least provide a filmed record of who opened the safe or deposit box.
4. The positioning of deposit boxes or vaults so that they may be observed easily by passing patrols.

Chapter 14

Fraud Against the Hotel

In addition to out-and-out robbery or theft, losses can occur from methods of fraud to which hotels are particularly vulnerable. It is a difficult subject to discuss realistically, as there are a variety of frauds which may be practiced, and also because a well-run hotel is very conscious of its public relations image. There may be a conflict between the desire to maintain good relations with the public who frequent the hotel, and the measures which may be used to lessen the chances of being defrauded. The methods of defrauding a hotel include:

1. Reserving a room and leaving without paying the bill for same.
2. Tendering "no account" or "insufficient funds" checks in payment for rooms, refreshments or other goods and supplies.
3. Obtaining accommodations, goods or services and requesting the hotel to charge the account to some business or institution later found to be nonexistent.
4. Booking accommodations at a single occupancy rate and then introducing other persons into the accommodations, thereby defrauding the hotel of the additional revenue it is entitled to receive for the extra guest(s).
5. Charging the hotel account to a stolen credit card.

There are some steps that can be taken to prevent such types of fraud without unduly disturbing the good public relations image of the hotel. All preventive measures will require the training of hotel staff in their proper application. These measures might include, among others, the following specific actions.

ROOM FRAUDS

"Skipping"

There are a number of "tip-offs" associated with "skippers"—those who obtain a room and depart without paying their bill. These acts should arouse suspicion but should not be considered a positive sign of fraud. The guest who arrives with no luggage should create some suspicion. In this case, the hotel should exercise its legal right to request payment for a room in advance. Quite often, a businessman may be caught in town late at night and, unable to get home, will go to a hotel. Naturally, since he was not planning on spending the night in town, he will have no luggage. His intentions are honorable, however, and he will normally not object to being asked politely to pay in advance. This practice is, or should be, standard operating procedure in motels, where the coming and going of guests cannot be as easily controlled.

Many "skippers" do not confine their stay to one night. They arrive with baggage, contract for a room for a number of days, and after they have enjoyed themselves for a period of time, they "take off." Often, these persons will really "live it up" during their stay and will charge every purchase or service to their account, including tips. They will frequent the barber shop, make purchases at the drug store, eat and drink the finest, and charge everything. A posting clerk or cashier noticing such activity would be wise to advise the credit manager or the security officer. Again, the hotel has the right to demand payment upon presentation of the bill. If management has real suspicions about a guest, they should not hesitate to confront him and request payment. It should be standard procedure that no hotel bill be allowed to run beyond one week before being presented for payment.

As was mentioned in Chapter 10 concerning thefts from hotel rooms, every attempt should be made to secure the license number of the guest's automobile. Even if the car is stolen, the license number may provide a good lead to the identity of the guest.

Registration Procedures

Many large hotels today ask the guest, at the time he registers, how the bill is to be paid—cash, check, credit card, or charge to a company. If a credit card is to be used, the card is inspected at that time and the number is imprinted directly on the guest folio (bill). If the name on the credit card does not agree with the name shown on the registration, the guest can be questioned. In addition, if the card contains the signature of the holder, this can be compared with his signature on the registration form. If the account is to be settled by check or charge to a company, there is sufficient time to check on the company or with the bank if there is any suspicion the guest is not legitimate. Some hotels have a policy whereby the guest making advance reservations is notified that if the account is to be paid by check, a letter of credit from the bank should be provided by the guest, or that the hotel reserves the right to telephone the bank at the guest's expense to verify the check's validity.

All of these procedures make it more difficult for the "skipper" to carry out his illegal activity. With false identification and a lot of poise and fast talk, however, the professional skipper can easily convince a registration clerk and even a credit manager. Skippers are normally professionals, and therefore are prepared for every contingency. They may act indignant or very humble when questioned. They may claim to be a personal friend of the manager. (This claim should be checked out immediately.) They will normally try everything and anything when backed into a corner. Anyone who seems to act or react too strongly should be considered suspicious.

Extra Persons in Room

Normally, extra persons in a room should be discovered by the maid who is required to make a room check each morning. These reports are returned to the housekeeper's office, where a master sheet is made up and forwarded to the front office. This report is checked against the room rack and any discrepancies are immediately investigated. The maid may report a room occupied while the room rack shows this room to be vacant, or vice versa. If the maid reports two occupants in a room where only one is registered, the registered occupant of the room should be contacted immediately.

When guests request that charges be placed on their accounts, these charges should be sent to the cashier as soon as possible so they may be entered on the guest's account. While late charges can be sent to a guest's address of record after his departure, it is an inconvenience for both parties and should be avoided as much as possible. The guest may refuse to pay the charge, or the address may be a false one. Although the charge may be small, it is still revenue that the hotel is entitled to receive.

Care must be taken that there is sufficient staff on hand at all hours of the day and night to accept money from guests desiring to settle their accounts regardless of the hour.

BAD CHECKS AND CREDIT FRAUD

Credit Cards

Credit cards are becoming more and more the accepted manner of doing business rather than handling cash. Consequently, incidents of credit card fraud are increasing. Many companies publish lists of stolen credit card numbers, and these lists should be checked to protect the hotel. Also, as we mentioned earlier, some companies maintain 'round-the-clock service offices where a particular card number may be checked. If suspicion is raised concerning a given card, a telephone call would be in order for the protection of the hotel.

Check-Cashing Procedures

In its desire to be of service to its guests, the hotel can encounter serious difficulties in accepting checks. No one can walk into a bank and cash a check on another bank, yet people expect a hotel to cash a check without question. The hotel should reserve the right to call the bank to ascertain the validity of the check before cashing it. If the check is presented for cashing on a weekend when the banks are closed, management must decide whether they wish to take the risk. Some guests will make the check out for a greater amount than their hotel account and request the difference in cash. The hotel should adopt a policy limiting the amount of cash that may be drawn under these circumstances.

Some hotels have installed a camera that takes a picture of the check and the person cashing the check. These machines are often used in banks, supermarkets and other public locations. One hotel has gone so far as to require a thumbprint of the person cashing the check to be applied with a new inkless print system. We would suggest that such precautions are necessary only if a large number of bad checks are being passed.

As can be seen, the question of fraud is a difficult one, although there is no doubt that it is practiced extensively. The precautions that we have indicated will be some deterrent, but probably the best security device in this area is a well-trained and vigilant staff who are suspicious of unusual occurrences connected with the behavior of guests and who are willing to do all in their power to prevent the occurrence of fraud.

Dishonest Cashiers

Not all fraud taking place at the office cashier's location is perpetrated by the guests. The greatest bulk of the hotel revenue passes through these cashiers, and the possibilities for juggling accounts, falsifying accounts and absconding with funds are numerous. Without question, these employees should be bonded. The accounting department auditors should perform their duties in a careful and diligent manner.

A case recently occurred in a hotel that experienced a large amount of late-night, one-night business. The night clerk, who acted as night auditor and cashier, would register a guest late at night, collect in advance and pocket the money, never making up a guest folio. Unfortunately, the serial numbers of the accounts were not checked, so even if a bill was made up and the hotel copy destroyed, the hotel was unaware of what had taken place. The clerk, however, neglected to destroy the registration card. A question developed concerning one guest and, while his registration card was located, the copy of his folio was not. A long and detailed investigation resulted in uncovering many similar incidents. While the investigators were never able to be certain they had uncovered all such incidents, an amount in excess of $15,000 was found to have been pocketed by this clerk in a period of two years. When confronted with the evidence, the clerk admitted his theft and the hotel was repaid by the bonding company.

As with other cashiers, the banks of the front office cashiers should be checked regularly. Normally, these banks are the largest used in the hotel and may be a temptation to a dishonest person. If a cashier is absent for an unexplained reason for more than two days, the bank should be checked immediately.

Counterfeits and Forgeries

One problem that is international in scope is that of counterfeit money and counterfeit or stolen traveler's checks. Normally, when a large "block" of traveler's checks has been stolen, the serial numbers are distributed to areas where they may be passed. If these serial numbers are published, they should be made available to all cashiers. Traveler's checks are provided with a space for countersigning. This countersigning is designed to be accomplished in view of the cashier. If the check presented is already countersigned, the cashier should be very suspicious and should refuse to accept it unless the signer is known to the cashier. With sufficient time and practice, the thief can forge an acceptable signature; with practice, the expert can do the same quickly and under pressure. Nevertheless, the countersignature should be accomplished in the presence of the cashier.

If large quantities of counterfeit money are in circulation, serial numbers will be published by law enforcement agencies, and these lists should be made available to cashiers. In addition, there are on the market inexpensive detection devices that will alert a cashier in most cases to a counterfeit bill regardless of national origin. Instructions should be provided to all cashiers as to what action is to be taken in the event a counterfeit bill or a stolen traveler's check or money order is received or suspected. While counterfeiting of money is usually undertaken in the smaller denominations of paper money, larger bills are sometimes presented. In a case several years ago in Canada, counterfeit dimes were being circulated. Cashiers should be constantly aware of counterfeiting in paper or coin, in any denomination.

SUMMARY

At best, fraud is usually discovered after it has been committed. The more information that is available, and the sooner the investigation is started, the better are the chances of apprehending the guilty party. Whether prosecution will be undertaken will depend on a number of factors . . . the size of the loss, the chances for restitution, the policy of the local law enforcement agencies, etc. It might be well to point out that not every bad check received or every "skipper" is an attempt to defraud the hotel. The person involved should be contacted and given the opportunity to make restitution. Quite often there is a misunderstanding or an error which is entirely unintentional. It is far better to give the guest at least a chance to make restitution before bringing a lawsuit or having him arrested.

Chapter 15

Fire and Disaster Protection

PRE-PLANNING FOR FIRE

Many hotels and motels advertise themselves as "fireproof" buildings. This is a dangerous misnomer—there is no such thing as a fireproof building. Concrete and steel will not burn by themselves, it is true, but inside that concrete and steel shell there is always a certain amount of wood, paper, cloth, electrical circuits and people. Although new fire-resistive materials, such as paints and carpeting, are being developed constantly, every hotel, motel, home or other building is filled with products that will burn and create toxic gases that can be even more deadly than the fire itself. It must be remembered that of the fire deaths in any given year throughout the world (over 12,000 in the United States alone), the greatest percentage of those victims die, not from burning, but from asphyxiation.

A fire, regardless of how small, in a hotel can be a tremendous disaster. Although the fire services throughout the world have conducted education programs for the public in what to do when fire strikes, most people do not know the correct procedures and either do nothing or do the wrong things. If people do not know what to do when fire occurs in their own homes, how can they be expected to do what is right when they are in strange surroundings such as a hotel? For this reason, it is the duty of management (and this will be a prime responsibility of the security officer) to ensure:

- That all fire safety regulations are observed to the letter.
- That fire hazards are removed.
- That the necessary and proper fire-fighting equipment is on hand.
- That alarm systems and extinguishing equipment are maintained in proper working condition.
- That in the event of fire, every employee, guest or visitor acts in the proper manner.

In order to accomplish all of this, pre-planning is essential and a good deal of inspection must be carried out. There is no greater hazard to contend with, and therefore there can be no room for indifference in the approach to fire safety.

Fire Codes

In most countries today, there are laws in effect that dictate, to a degree, what standards must be met in hotels, motels or other buildings where the general public may seek accommodations. In many cases these regulations are very strict, while others may be less demanding. The degree of enforcement may also vary, as will the penalties for non-compliance. Most of the United States and Canada have had laws regarding fire safety and inspection systems in effect for a number of years. In 1972, legislation was introduced in Britain requiring inspection of all hotels or rooming houses after application for a fire safety certificate. The establishments are not permitted to operate without this certificate and the penalties are severe.

While these regulations set certain standards and requirements, it must be remembered that these are minimum standards. There is nothing to prevent the innkeeper from providing greater safety than what may be required by law. It would be well for the security officer to determine what regulations apply in his location and base his initial fire prevention survey on the applicable standards.

Fire Doors

We have already mentioned fire doors as they apply to entry of unauthorized persons into the hotel (Chapter 7), but further consideration is needed. Normally, fire and building codes or life safety codes will regulate only the type of construction of the door, requiring that it will be self-closing and that there be no lock or locking device that will impede exit through that door. If there is any glass in the door, it must be limited in amount and must be wired glass or material capable of withstanding heat in excess of that found in normal window glass.

The purpose of a fire door, and in particular of the panic hardware on such a door, is to comply with the requirement that *exit or egress is always available,* while persons are prevented from entering from the outside through this means of exit. A door provided with a lock in the knob, which is always open on the exit side but can only be opened from the opposite side with a key, does not give the desired protection. Locks can be "picked" and keys can be duplicated. In addition, such a door has only one point of locking, where the bolt of the knob lock enters the door frame. On a fire door equipped with panic hardware, there may be three or more points where the door is secured to the frame.

It is recommended that doors leading to fire towers be labeled clearly "EMERGENCY EXIT ONLY—Exit from this stairway at ground level only." If it is desired that such a stairway be made available as an access stairway between various floors, it is *imperative* that the ground floor exit from the stairway be equipped with panic hardware so that entry cannot be made from the outside. Any or all doors may be equipped with alarms so that, if they are opened for any reason, a signal is given and the reason for the opening may be investigated. If it is not desired to alarm each door, the lower portion of the stairway may be provided with a motion sensor that will indicate when someone is in the area. Without such precautions, it is obvious that undesirables can come and go as they please in this stairway.

Inspections Needed

Normally, fire insurance rates are based on the condition of the property, taking into account a number of factors. For that reason, the building will be inspected by representatives of the Rating Bureau as well as representatives of the insurance company. Management or the security officer would do well to heed the recommendations of these officials. Doing so may result not only in increased protection but also in a decreased insurance rate.

The local fire department is usually more than willing to assist in surveying the property to point out hazards and make recommendations. An invitation to the fire department to inspect the building serves two very important functions: not only can these professionals point out hazards and make suggestions, but they will have an opportunity to become familiar with the physical layout of the building. Fire departments spend a great deal of time in pre-planning, so that, if they must respond to an alarm, they know what is involved and the location of the essential services, fire-fighting equipment, special hazards, etc. A smoke-filled street in the dark of night is not the place to be searching for a sprinkler standpipe connection. The closer the cooperation between the hotel and the fire department, the better for all concerned.

If the hotel is located in an area served by a volunteer fire department, these persons may not have had the training necessary to carry out a proper fire prevention survey. In these cases the hotel's fire insurance agent may be able to help.

THE FIRE PREVENTION SURVEY

When the fire prevention and protection survey is conducted, whether by the security officer alone or in the company of fire officials or insurance representatives, what should be the main concerns? While entire books have been written on this subject, we will attempt to cover some of the most important aspects of such a survey.

Housekeeping

The general condition of the building from a standpoint of housekeeping should be noted. Trash and dirt must not be allowed to accumulate. Storage areas must be kept neat and tidy so that access is not impaired. Flammable substances, such as paints and painting supplies, oils and other lubricants, must be stored properly in fire-resistive cabinets. Rags and other items that might be used in connection with these flammable substances must be stored in a metal can with a lid. No great accumulation of these items should be permitted.

Fire Regulations

It must be determined what fire regulations are in effect and the degree of compliance with these regulations. Certain areas in the back of the house should be designated "no smoking" areas. In fact, smoking by employees should be limited to very specific areas such as the cafeteria, locker room or some area of low hazard. If cigarette butts are observed throughout hallways, elevator cabs and in storage areas, it is obvious that smoking restrictions are not being observed. Management should take immediate action to enforce the "no smoking" rules. Cigarettes and smoking materials are still the number one cause of fires.

Fire doors designed to be kept closed should be inspected to be sure they are closed at all times. Often a door will be blocked open to provide ventilation or ease in passing, but in the event of a fire, this open door could permit smoke and toxic gases to pass from one area to another with great speed. Doors that are normally open at all times, but are equipped with a fusible link set to allow the door to close in the event of a fire, must be tested periodically to ensure the door will close properly when the fuse is released. Through inactivity over a period of time, these doors sometimes become stuck. If a track is involved, the track may become filled with dirt, preventing the door from closing all the way.

Extinguishing Equipment

The availability and maintenance of fire-fighting equipment must be checked. Usually there are regulations specifying the amount of equipment necessary and the placement of same. If such regulations do not exist, the recommendations of the National Fire Protection Association (or its counterparts in Canada or Great Britain) can be used. It must be remembered that there are four classes of fires, three of which will be involved in a hotel. The extinguishing agent recommended for each class is different, so we must consider what type of fire is most likely to occur and be certain that we have the proper extinguisher for that class.

Class A – These fires involve the burning of normal combustible materials such as wood, paper, etc. Normally such fires are extinguished by cooling the materials below the combustion temperature, and this can be accomplished with water. A pressurized water extinguisher or a soda and acid extinguisher may be used safely.

Class B – Such fires involve flammable or combustible liquids, flammable gases, greases and similar materials. Water cannot be used in such an instance as it would tend to spread the fire. A smothering action is required to extinguish a Class B fire, so carbon dioxide or dry chemical may be used.

Class C – Fires of this nature involve energized electrical equipment. Again, if water is used, a severe electrical shock might result, since water is a conductor of electricity. Carbon dioxide or dry powder must be used.

Class D – This refers to fire in combustible metals such as titanium or magnesium. These are unlikely in most hotels. The only effective extinguishing agent against a Class D fire is a special chemical powder.

Foam extinguishers are available, as well as an all-purpose dry powder, that may be used on Class A, B or C fires. The use of the pyrene or carbon tetrachloride extinguisher has been outlawed in many places and is not recommended due to the danger of highly toxic fumes developing in restricted areas. If such extinguishers are presently available to guests or employees, they should be removed immediately.

Recently, a new extinguishing agent, Halon 1301, has become available. This is an inert gas, delivered under pressure. Available as installed tanks and nozzles or as a portable fire extinguisher, it is very rapid, non-toxic, and is suitable for Class A, B or C fires. Although it is rather expensive, its use is spreading rapidly, particularly in complex electrical installations such as computers.

The type of extinguisher to be provided will depend on the type of fire expected and the economics of purchasing. An all-purpose extinguisher costs more than a pressurized water unit which will handle a Class A fire very well. Too much equipment, or the wrong equipment, can hurt the overall program.

Where equipment is designed to operate under pressure, inspections must be made to be sure pressure is maintained. Carbon dioxide extinguishers must be weighted periodically, sprinkler systems checked, hoses tested and repacked to prevent cracking. All equipment must be maintained in first-class condition at all times.

Two very important points must be stressed in this connection. First, if there is a sprinkler system in the building, the main valve for this system should be equipped with some form of lock so that the valve cannot be closed. If repairs must be made to the system and the valve must be closed, the insurance company should be notified and the repairs made as quickly as possible. Once the repairs are completed, the valve should be opened again and locked in the open position.

It is strongly recommended that the standpipe system, the sprinkler system and all valves supplying them be a supervised system which notifies some responsible authority of any change from normal operating status. For example, if a supply valve is closed, an alarm would be registered; if a sprinkler activates and water begins to flow, an alarm would be sounded and the situation can be immediately investigated. Many buildings which were equipped with sprinkler systems have burned to the ground because someone closed the supply valve, inadvertently or on purpose. With a supervised system, this cannot occur.

Secondly, the fire department should be asked to inspect the standpipe system in the hotel to ensure that the threads on the outlets are of the same thread as the fire department hoses. It would be unfortunate indeed if the fire department attempted to connect to a sprinkler standpipe or any standpipe only to find a different thread preventing them from making a connection. If it is known in advance that a difference exists, the proper adaptors can be provided.

Electrical Systems

The condition of electrical systems in the hotel is important. While a casual visual inspection will probably be inconclusive, some violations may be noted, such as overloading outlets, worn cords, or overheated lines. Fuses should be of the proper size; where continual breakdowns occur, the system should be checked out. Where spray painting may be done or where fumes may exist, explosion-proof motors should be installed. Inspection and maintenance of the electrical distribution system should be left to the experts, the electrical engineers; however, the basic preventive measures can be handled by all concerned—worn cords, cords run under rugs, broken switches, etc. These hazards, when observed by any employee, should be reported.

Employee Training

The training and instructions given employees should be noted in the survey. Do all employees know what to do in the event of a fire—how to report a fire, how to operate an extinguisher? Are drills held occasionally and are refresher courses given employees? These are questions that must be asked and answered so that planning can take place to correct deficiencies.

Instructions to Guests

The provisions to notify guests in the event of fire and the instructions available to ensure that guests react in the proper manner should be reviewed. Some form of alarm system—a fire bell or other audible signal—should be in effect. Too often, however, that is where the system ends. There are no instructions to the guest as to what he is supposed to do when he hears the alarm bell. Some areas require that instructions be posted on the back of every guest room door, indicating what the occupant should do in the event of a fire alarm, and showing the location of the fire exit nearest that particular room. These instructions should be as simple as possible, as clear as possible and printed in type large enough to be read easily. Fire officials should assist in compiling these instructions. Instructions should also be posted in large letters at elevator landings that elevators *are not to be used* in the event of fire.

Reporting Systems

Fire reporting systems must be taken into account. It is strongly recommended that any "pull stations" located within the building be connected to an annunciator board in the security office or at some other location with 24-hour coverage, with an additional direct line to the municipal fire department. Too often such alarm boxes are proprietary alarms only and the fire department is not notified as soon as desirable. The internal annunciator board would give the exact location of the "box" involved, while the direct line to the fire department would indicate the building location only. There should be a capability of manually ringing any or all fire bells in the building from a central control point so that planned evacuation can be undertaken.

Warnings

As a matter of public relations, it may be advisable to place in each guest room an attractive tent card or eye-catching sign reminding the occupants of the danger of fire and suggesting that they refrain from smoking in bed. Such comments as "If you smoke in bed, the ashes on the floor may be your own," or "We want to see you again, so please don't go out in smoke," together with an appropriate cartoon, might help prevent a hazardous situation.

The fire prevention survey will indicate how extensive and how efficient the hotel's prevention program is. The security officer can then make recommendations to management for improvements, new regulations and new equipment if necessary. Careful attention must be given to the high hazard areas—the kitchens, where most hotel fires occur due to the hazard of grease, fats, and oils being ignited, and guest or public areas where smoking is permitted at all times. Regulations and preventive measures must be instituted in these areas. Employees must be made fire-conscious and must be trained to recognize and report hazards. Then, realizing that fires will still occur no matter how good a prevention program may be, the hotel must develop a plan of action to be followed.

FIRE BILL

The Fire Bill is no more than a written plan setting forth what is to be done when a fire is reported or discovered, how it is to be done, and who is to do it. The plan is made available to every employee involved so that each person knows what is expected of him. The following would be among the points that should be covered in such a plan.

Reporting a Fire

The Fire Bill should give specific and detailed instructions on how to report a fire and to whom to report it, and what follow-up action is to be taken. For example, "Upon discovering a fire, go to the nearest telephone and advise the operator that there is a fire, give the location specifically and clearly. If you are near a fire alarm box, this box may be activated; however, a call should still be placed to the operator. Above all, *stay calm.*

"After the alarm has been given, return to the fire scene and attempt to extinguish it if possible, or, if there are guests in the immediate area who might be in danger, conduct them to safety."

Operator Action

The specific action that the telephone operator is to take should be spelled out in the Fire Bill. Most important, naturally, should be to notify the fire department immediately, giving a clear and exact location of the fire. Additional instructions should include who else is to be notified—management, maintenance, security, engineering, etc.

Personnel Assignments

The Fire Bill should make clear the specific action that each person or department notified is to take. For example, "Maintenance men are to report to the scene of the fire with hand tools, hand lights and extra extinguishers. Engineering will start house pumps (if connected to standpipe system). Security will go to street to await fire department and escort them directly to the fire scene and provide such pass keys as are necessary to ensure easy entry into any location."

It is not advisable to assign duties by name, such as "John Jones will. . . ." It is preferable to designate by title, such as "the duty engineer" or "all housemen on duty" so that, regardless of turnover, the plan will be effective and each person will know his or her duties.

Certain job titles should be designated responsibility for reporting to areas of the hotel to direct and assist guests if evacuation is required. This will prevent panic and make the entire operation most efficient and probably more rapid. Care must be taken that provisions are made for 24-hour coverage and that those employees involved in this operation receive proper instruction and training.

New employees should be carefully instructed as to what their duties may be and, most importantly, how to report a fire.

Night Inspections

Inspection for fire hazards at night should be provided for in the Fire Bill. Night watchmen and other night personnel should be trained and instructed to check soft furniture, sofas, chesterfields and other furniture in public spaces for discarded or dropped cigarettes when first reporting for duty and after the normal traffic of the day subsides.

Room Record

An up-to-date room count sheet should be kept available at all times so that immediate information is available as to what rooms are occupied in the event evacuation is required. A check can then be made to ensure that all occupants have vacated the building.

Normally, fire alarms are sounded inside the hotel only when it is desirable to evacuate the entire building. This would not be the case in a small fire confined to one room or area. The decision to evacuate the building and to ring the internal fire alarm bells should rest with the chief of the Municipal Fire Department. In addition, today's multi-story high-rise buildings do not call for total evacuation. It will be the decision of the Fire Chief in command which floors are to be evacuated. Under such conditions, it becomes almost a necessity that alarm bells be zoned so that only those involved need be sounded. (Evacuation is discussed in more detail in Chapter 16.)

The problems connected with fire and fire prevention cannot be stressed too strongly. The hazard of fire exists constantly in spite of all precautions that might be taken, and we must therefore be prepared at all times. Nighttime comes and the hazard increases as there are fewer people on hand to discover fires. Security must be increased during these hours.

Fire Department Assistance

The local fire department is more than willing to assist and advise in any way possible with the hotel fire protection and prevention program, from inspections to training personnel in the handling of extinguishers. Any fire department is more interested in *preventing* fires than in fighting them. Do not hesitate to make use of their talents *before* fire occurs as well as when fire occurs.

Drills Needed

Finally, it must be realized that, even though a perfect plan may be formulated and reduced to writing, if the people responsible for implementing the plan are not instructed in their duties, if there are no actual tests conducted and no drills held, the value of the entire system is questionable. People do not have time to stop, find a manual and read the instructions when an emergency occurs. Their actions must come without delay and this can only be accomplished through actual training. Alarm bells do not have to be sounded, but conditions can be simulated and employees can indicate what their reaction would be under given conditions. It would be advisable, however, for the bells to be tested on occasion to ensure that no faults have developed in the system. Advance notice can be given to guests of such a test in order to avoid confusion or panic.

ARSON

Organized Crime Involvement

Arson is sometimes relied upon by organized crime to further their aims. For example, a businessman unwilling to "cooperate" with the syndicate may find his establishment the victim of the "torch." The victim of a loanshark deal, unable to pay the interest let alone repay the principal, may burn his business in order to collect the insurance to settle the account. The arsonist may be provided by the syndicate.

Financial Trouble as Motive

Not all arson, however, is associated with organized crime. Many businessmen, finding themselves in financial difficulties due to economic conditions, outdated properties, changes in population centers or decline of neighborhoods, may decide to "sell" their business to the insurance companies. Resort areas which have suffered a bad season due to poor weather or other causes may well "resort" to arson to solve their problems. While professional "torches" are available through underworld connections, many amateurs are also involved, and professional as well as amateur arson rings are prevalent throughout the world. The increase in arson or suspicious fires over the past ten years has been tremendous, and the hotel industry has not been overlooked in this increase. Additional motives in hotel arson include revenge by an employee with a grievance, and vandalism.

Hotel Arson Incidents

Probably the most serious hotel arson occurred in Quebec in 1973. Several hotels were burned, all of them involving insurance frauds by organized crime. Two other peculiar incidents have occurred in Ontario, Canada. The first one concerned a hotel in Toronto where six small fires were set in quick succession by an aggrieved employee. The fires occurred in linen closets and similar locations and were contained by the sprinkler system. No casualties occurred. The second incident concerned an old hotel which had been stripped and was scheduled for demolition. It was burned down and arson was established as the cause. In view of the fact that the insurance had been allowed to lapse and this fact had been publicized, vandalism appeared to be the only logical explanation.

DISASTER PROTECTION

Many areas of the world are subject to disasters such as floods, hurricanes, tornadoes, earthquakes, cyclones or severe snow and rain storms. In some cases, there will be advance warnings of such incidents to permit precautions to be taken. At other times the incident can occur without warning. The hotel must be prepared to do whatever is necessary to protect property and provide for the safety of all persons within the hotel. Based on previous experience in a given location, plans can be made in advance as to what action should be taken in the event of such an emergency. For example, coastal areas susceptible to hurricanes should plan what action is to be taken when a hurricane is expected to reach the area. Other areas may never experience a hurricane but may be in tornado country and should preplan what action is to be taken.

Detailed Planning

It is hoped that these disasters will never happen, of course, but it is better to be prepared and to know exactly what is to be done and who is responsible for doing it, than to wait until the last minute and be forced to take action in a confused and inefficient manner. Often, if preplanning has taken place, measures can be taken in a quiet and unobtrusive manner that will not disturb the guests or cause unnecessary concern or panic. Just as in the case of the Fire Bill, the details of what is to be done must be spelled out clearly, setting forth the responsibilities of each employee, again by job title. Some additional thoughts that should go into disaster planning would be:

1. Special supplies—plywood for boarding up windows, ice- and snow-removing equipment, portable pumps, etc.—should be purchased in advance and kept on hand.

2. Provisions should be made for housing and feeding employees unable to leave the building due to weather conditions, or whom management desires to retain on the premises.

3. Fresh water supplies should be stocked in the event the public water system is damaged.

4. Provisions for emergency lighting are needed in the event electric power is lost. This can include anything from an emergency generator to a supply of candles.

5. Various degrees of action to be taken should be spelled out. For example, in the case of a hurricane, the first warnings are sometimes issued days in advance. At that time all that might be required is that a check be made to be certain that necessary supplies are on hand. At a later time when more precise information is received and the hurricane watch becomes a hurricane warning, additional steps can be taken, such as the removal and storage of outside furniture, the securing or removing of boats, etc. Finally, when it is apparent that the storm is about to hit, the final precautions such as boarding up windows can be accomplished.

Whatever is done should be accomplished calmly so as not to disrupt normal operations or cause undue concern among the guests. They certainly should be kept informed of what is occurring in the event they wish to make plans of their own for leaving the area.

Civil Defense

In addition to the incidents we have already mentioned, the world is still concerned with possible acts of war and many hotels have been designated shelter areas in the event of nuclear attack. Plans for such emergencies should be made in cooperation with local, state or federal Civil Defense Agencies. It should also be pointed out that hotels can play the same role in the event of a local catastrophe. The hotel may be asked to house, feed and otherwise care for disaster victims. Again, preplanning of how to handle such incidents will be invaluable. The plan should be a part of the hotel's security program and should be reviewed from time to time as situations and conditions change.

Chapter 16

Special Security Situations

BOMB THREATS

A bomb threat is a serious problem now facing many industries and institutions. Typically, a telephone call is received from an unknown source stating that a bomb has been planted in the building. Advance planning is required to handle such an incident properly. The local, state or provincial police can be of great assistance in this planning. Recommendations by authorities concerning such matters apply to all establishments and can be adopted by hotels. Briefly, these recommendations include such items as the following.

Handling the Threat

1. Detailed recording by the person receiving the threat of exactly what was said. Every attempt should be made to have the caller say as much as possible in the hope that he will indicate where the bomb is planted, when it is to go off, why it was placed in the hotel, etc. The more information that can be gathered, the better are the chances of locating the bomb, if in fact there is one on the premises. Attention should also be given to listening for any clues as to the identity or location of the caller. Accents, tone quality, and background noises should be noted and referred to the proper authorities.

2. Notify the police as soon as possible, as well as management and the security department.
3. Provide small groups of search personnel to work with police and/or fire officials. Designate areas to be searched by specific teams made up of those persons most familiar with the areas.

Decision to Evacuate

Depending on the nature of the threat and local conditions at the time, the decision will have to be made whether the building is to be evacuated or not. This is normally a decision that rests entirely with the building owner or his designated representative. Naturally, police officials will offer advice, and it would be well for the hotel manager to seek and heed such advice. Often the police have more information on the current situation and are better prepared to judge the validity of the threat. The final decision, however, still rests in the hands of the building owner or his representative.

Many bomb threats have been made against hotels. Every innkeeper and security officer must consider that it can happen to his establishment, and he must be prepared in advance to handle the situation.

Evacuation/Take-Cover Plan

Since the need for evacuation of a hotel may arise due to the threat of fire or a bomb threat, plans must be formulated in advance as to how such an operation is to be handled. Many factors must be considered, including maximum number of persons expected to be within the building at a given time, the location of those persons, the number and location of elevators, the number and location of stairwells, the location of the building core(s), the number of disabled, elderly or nonambulatory persons on the property, the construction of the building, the exposures of the building. These and many other factors must be weighed in any plan considered. In the planning of such an operation, it would be well to secure assistance from professionals dealing with such problems.

Asking guests or tenants to remain in their rooms might be

sensible in some situations. If this is the case, there must be available a means of communicating with the guests as quickly as possible as well as with the employees who will be required to assist in the operation. The communications system may range from a bull-horn at the least (with questionable results), to the use of any public address systems within the building, closed circuit television if available, or (probably the best method) a system whereby all telephones can be activated at the same time with a recorded message transmitted as the instrument is answered in each room. Instructions can be given as to exactly what action is desired of the room occupant. For years, many brave and dedicated telephone operators stayed by their switchboards calling each room individually in an attempt to warn the occupants of impending danger. Thanks to advances in the telephone system, such procedures are no longer required and the entire operation can be handled in a matter of minutes.

Evacuation and take-cover plans are difficult at best to formulate. Serious pre-planning must be accomplished to be successful in that once-in-a-lifetime case when they will be required. The best advice for the hotel is to secure reliable professional help in this planning.

SPECIAL EVENTS

There are a number of occasions which will require security above and beyond that normally provided on a day-to-day basis. Such occasions may arise due to the presence of a VIP as a guest or as an attendee at a function. This could be a political figure such as a president, prime minister, member of royalty, or a political candidate, or it could be a famous person from the arts, letters, sciences or whatever. Another occasion requiring extra security might be the presence of a group of controversial nature such as a political convention, a convention of activists or union leaders or members, or perhaps simply a group with a reputation for being boisterous.

VIP Protection

At a time when political assassination, assassination attempts and kidnapings plague almost every nation in the world, the security measures by all law enforcement agencies have been increased when political figures make public appearances. Naturally, the more prominent the personality, the more protection is required. In some cases, it is necessary to protect well-known persons not only from intentional harm but also from over-zealous fans or followers. In any case, the cooperation and assistance of local police will probably be necessary, and in the case of very important figures of state, the federal and state or provincial law enforcement agencies will be involved and will take charge of the security measures to a great degree. The role of the hotel then becomes one of complete cooperation, assisting those in command in any way possible.

Under such circumstances the hotel security officer is usually assigned to work directly with the officer or officers in charge. The outside agencies do not know the layout of the hotel and are unfamiliar with the employees and the facilities available. Some of the considerations that may have to be resolved by all concerned will include:

1. "Back door" entrance and exit for VIPs to avoid crowds at main entrance.

2. Exposure protection. If sleeping accommodations are to be used by VIPs, the control of those rooms adjacent to and above or below the VIP's room and, if necessary, in adjacent buildings, must be considered.

If a VIP accompanied by a sizable party is to be present for one or more nights, it is good policy to reserve an entire floor for the group. This simplifies the security problem, as it is obviously easier to secure an entire floor where no other persons require access, than would be the case where other guests, not in the official party, require access to their rooms on the same floor.

3. Provision for necessary facilities—not only accommodations for VIP and staff, but also provision of special telephones, teletypes, etc.

4. Establishment of command center and adequate personnel to operate it.

5. Identification and security checks on employees.

6. Traffic and parking requirements.

7. Control of guests and other occupants of the building to ensure safety, privacy and well-being of persons being protected.

8. Necessary supervision of food preparation and service. If

special diets or cooking procedures are to be followed, or if specific cooking and serving utensils are required, the necessary arrangements must be made. In some instances, a "taster" may be required to sample all foods before they are served to prevent any chance of poisoning.

While it is difficult to set forth rules to be followed in such instances, as each case will have to be handled according to its particular circumstances, it might help to relate the security details to two personal experiences of the authors . . . one concerning a United States National Governors' Conference and the other a National Political (Presidential) Convention.

Example: Governors' Conference

The annual Governors' Conference is hosted by the governor of the state where the meeting is held. It is his responsibility to make all arrangements and plans aside from the agenda of the meetings. The meeting related here took place in New Jersey. The Commanding Officer of the New Jersey State Police was placed in charge of security details. Months before the conference, meetings were held with this officer and his aides, the local chief of police and the hotel security officer. Every detail was discussed, physical arrangements were made so that, at the time of the conference, all was in readiness. Sufficient State Police officers were assigned to provide each governor with an officer around the clock. The officer acted as bodyguard, chauffeur, messenger, personal aide, etc. In addition, officers were available to do door duty at any conferences or meeting sessions to ensure privacy.

A command post was established in a convenient office and was equipped with emergency telephones, radio communications and such other equipment as was deemed necessary. This post was manned around the clock, and all matters relating to security and security details were channeled through this office.

In addition, six teams were established, each consisting of a state police officer, a municipal police officer and a hotel security officer. Two of these teams were in service at all times and were charged with the overall security of the property. They made patrols throughout the building on an unscheduled basis, watching for undesirable persons or security hazards. The hotel representative naturally was familiar with the building and its employees, the local police officer was familiar with the local "characters," and the State Police officer from the intelligence unit was familiar with known "troublemakers" from other parts of the state or country. Together, this team was able to account for almost every person in the building. If any suspicion arose, they had the authority to stop and question and, if necessary, detain a subject.

The conference was a success from the security standpoint, since there were no incidents to disrupt the meeting. There is no way to determine whether this would have been true if these precautions had not been taken; we can only assume that things ran smoothly because this added protection was present.

National Political Convention

A National Political Presidential Convention presents further problems. In the first place, far more people are involved, the convention attracts many more outsiders, the delegates and candidates are spread out over a far wider area, and there is more movement of persons. Normally, the candidates themselves are provided with protection so this does not become a problem for the hotel. The biggest problem is controlling the people who desire to reach the candidate; these may be individuals or large groups. It can be a quiet, simple approach or it can be a violent, riotous confrontation such as occurred during the Democratic convention in Chicago in 1968. A great deal of pre-planning is necessary, and complete cooperation between the law enforcement agencies involved and the hotel is most important. The local police are usually spread rather thin during such an event, and duties such as guarding entrances to meetings must be left to contract guard services. Identification is vital so that plainclothes security officers can identify and be identified by plainclothes law enforcement officers. This can be done by small lapel badges.

As far as the hotel is concerned, an event such as a political convention should be handled like any other busy day with simply more security provided. Those in the hotel are expected to behave in an orderly manner and it is the responsibility of the hotel to see that they do, but if matters get out of hand, the hotel should request assistance from other law enforcement agencies. The police should not enter the hotel without the permission and approval of management unless it is an extreme emergency.

During the convention in which the author was involved, a command post was set up in the hotel with adequate staff to man it around the clock. A convention command post was established in the city where representatives of all law enforcement agencies involved were located. Messages could be transmitted easily to and from the hotel. If an unscheduled event was to take place, such as the visit of a top candidate or the incumbent President, word could be passed immediately and the necessary arrangements made. As was the case with the Governors' Conference, roving teams of officers were constantly on duty and ready to prevent any security hazard before it had an opportunity to get started.

Although incidents resulting in arrests did occur and there were some "touchy" situations, no serious or dangerous conditions were allowed to develop. The pre-planning and cooperation exhibited by all paid off to the satisfaction of all concerned.

When security is required for a given event beyond the normal day-by-day routine, we cannot over-emphasize the need for pre-planning. Sufficient personnel should be on hand or immediately available to assist the normal staff. We have witnessed a number of events that had the potential of becoming dangerous situations where a large force of officers was held out of sight but in the immediate vicinity to be called upon only if needed. The best method yet of preventing trouble is to stop it before it starts. To accomplish that, sufficient personnel must be immediately available. Then, by sheer numbers, violence can often be averted.

Security for Business Meetings

On occasion, a hotel may be chosen as the site for important business meetings where complete security is essential. The degree of security desired should be checked with those responsible for arranging the meeting. Services to be provided by the hotel should be reduced to writing.

It may be necessary for the hotel to provide airtight security, which would require the removal of telephones from the conference room, the electronic searching of the room to detect "bugs" or other electronic or audio surveillance devices, the blacking out of windows to prevent the use of infrared or lasers, and the soundproofing, as far as possible, of all doors and walls. This may sound like over-insurance, but news of important meetings often leaks out in advance and a hotel is very accessible to potential "bug planters." This fact should be realized by management and admitted freely to the conference organizer so he may request the security he feels his group requires.

If the hotel does not wish to become involved in such extensive security measures or does not have the facilities to provide such a service, the conference organizer should be so advised. If desired, he may contract with his own security force or specialist, thereby releasing the hotel from any responsibility other than "normal" or "reasonable" security.

CIVIL UNREST AND STRIKES

Civil disturbance is another common occurrence plaguing many cities and countries today. The reasons for racial or political unrest must be left to those who study such matters. Our concern is the protection of property and the lives of those within the hotel.

Hotel Can Be Target

Normally, the targets of rioters are neighborhood liquor stores, clothing stores, appliance or drug stores; however, hotels are by no means immune from such actions. If there are stores on the street level of the hotel, they may be subject to damage. Under such conditions, the local police are usually very busy and may not be able to respond to render assistance due to a manpower shortage or inability to reach the hotel. The hotel must rely on its own abilities and manpower. Just as we prepared for storms and fire, we must pre-plan and be prepared for this type of disturbance.

Protective Procedures

Some things that might be considered include:

1. Boarding up windows in stores on street levels.
2. Removal of liquor from street level stores or bars.
3. Securing of all entrances to the hotel except the main entrance, which should be manned by security personnel.

4. Providing lights, fire-fighting equipment and, if possible, personnel in stores at street level and on roofs where incendiary devices might be thrown.
5. Securing all engineering spaces to prevent unauthorized entry. If water supplies, electrical generating stations or similar facilities are part of the hotel mechanical operation and are located in adjacent buildings, adequate protection for such locations should be provided. (These should be fenced in or properly secured and provided with some form of alarm system long before a situation of civil unrest develops.)
6. Providing accommodations for employees who do not wish to return to their homes or who cannot leave the hotel without encountering personal danger.
7. If outside fire escapes are available, providing personnel to watch these escapes to prevent illegal entry into hotel.
8. Establishing a command post and maintaining close communication with all security personnel in service.
9. If possible, arranging for additional manpower through a contract security agency.

Once again, a show of strength is often a deterrent to a rowdy. Firearms, however, should not be displayed by hotel security personnel but should be left to the law enforcement officers.

Effects of A Strike

Many hotels today find themselves faced with a strike by union members. A number of unions may represent various employees within a given institution; despite the fact that only one union may strike, the other unions may honor the picket lines of the striking union and refuse to enter the premises. The presence of picket lines may also curtail deliveries to the establishment, cutting off the delivery of food and other supplies. In addition to curtailed services and supplies, violence and sabotage may occur with or without the sanction or approval of union officials.

Security personnel will be faced with the responsibility of

protecting the hotel property. As in the case of civil disturbances, special attention should be paid to vital areas where sabotage could cause serious problems. In addition, security personnel should maintain complete and accurate records of all events or occurrences relative to picketing to support any legal action such as application for an injunction. In the event that violence does take place, police protection may be offered or made available, and the security officer will be required to coordinate his staff with the officers assigned to the hotel. Protection must also be provided for those employees not involved in the strike or not sympathetic with the strikers. Where possible, room and board must be provided for those employees who refuse to leave the premises for fear of violence against them or whose presence in the hotel is vital during the period of trouble.

Maintaining Order

Strikes are unfortunate situations and usually will leave scars by way of hard feelings at least. Care must be taken to maintain law and order at all times without allowing personal feelings or opinions to rule the situation. The conflict that leads to a strike is a matter between the employees and management and must be settled by these parties. The security officer must confine his efforts to the protection of the hotel property and the lives of all persons in or upon the premises.

A camera is a valuable tool during such an incident if damage is being done to the hotel's property. Many times the mere fact that strikers know photographs are being taken will be enough of a deterrent to prevent damage. The same camera can also be used by the security officer in many other situations and investigations and can be an important and valuable security tool. Pocket tape recorders are also valuable for rapid recording of events as they happen. The tapes can be transcribed later and will prove extremely useful if security officers are required to testify in court to support an application for an injunction to control violence by strikers.

SUMMARY

In any special situation, the chances of maintaining adequate security depend on the amount of pre-planning that has been accomplished. There are occasions when a situation will develop on the spur of the moment, but for the most part, all possibilities can be determined in advance and some plan of action prepared. Tact, restraint, common sense, a knowledge of the facilities and assistance available and a willingness to request such help, as well as an ability to "keep cool," will normally see a security officer through any difficult situation. It must be remembered that the prime function of the security officer and his department is to prevent trouble and to protect life and property.

Chapter 17

Organized Crime and the Hotel Industry

Some readers may conclude from the title of this chapter that it does not concern them because the property they represent is not involved in any way with organized crime. We plead with anyone under that impression that they read further, as there are phases of organized crime that touch almost every business to a degree. The comments here apply to the United States, Canada, and certain islands.

STRUCTURE OF ORGANIZED CRIME

Cosa Nostra

Organized crime as it operates today is known by many as the "Mafia," but more correctly it is the "Cosa Nostra." The organization in many respects is the same as it has been since the days of Prohibition in the United States. "Families" are located in various areas in the United States and Canada, and these groups control many of the illegal activities that operate within their geographic boundaries. The entire organization, consisting of the various Families, is governed by a group known as the Commissione that could be compared to a board of directors. The Commissione's main function is to keep the Cosa Nostra a going concern. It is the final arbiter on disputes between Families, and when a "Boss" (a leader of a Family) dies, it must confirm the man who takes his place.

Trend Away from Violence

In the past few years, the Cosa Nostra has attempted to eliminate the obvious "rough stuff" and rely more on brains than brawn to accomplish its end results. There are occasional murders and physical violence, but such publicity is not to the liking of the Commissione or many of the "Bosses" who desire to appear as legitimate businessmen involved in legitimate enterprises. The fact remains, however, that the same businesses are being conducted as in previous years in addition to a few new enterprises. Among the profit-making operations are numbers writing, bookmaking, other forms of gambling, loan sharking, prostitution, hijacking and black market operations. This is by no means the full extent of organized crime activities, but only some of the fields that may involve hotel operations.

While the Cosa Nostra may be involved in drug traffic, they do not approve of their own members using drugs. In the same respect, while they may be involved in other activities to cheat the public, they do not usually become direct participants. Very seldom does a numbers operator play the numbers himself, for example.

Ownership May Be Hidden

It is a fact that many apparently legitimate businesses, including hotels, are actually owned or controlled by members of the Cosa Nostra. The actual ownership is sometimes hidden, but not in all cases. The fact remains that if a hotel is owned by a "Family" or "Family" member, they desire it to be run in an economical manner and will take every precaution to maintain their legitimacy. The difference in operations from legitimately owned hotels will occur in the handling of profits, paying of taxes and similar areas which will not involve the security officer.

AREAS OF INVOLVEMENT

Numbers Writing

While a hotel itself may have no organized crime connection, its employees provide a fertile field for illegal activities because of the low average income associated with such employment. Numbers writing is usually widespread in a hotel, especially in urban areas where large numbers of active participants are located in a confined area. Normally the numbers writer is not an outsider who enters the hotel to make his daily bid for business, but is an employee who ends up devoting more time to writing numbers than to performing the services the hotel is paying him to accomplish.

One might ask why the hotel should worry about a few people playing the numbers. If an employee is devoting his time to gambling while the hotel pays him a salary to do a certain job which is not getting done, the hotel is wasting that salary. One might also ask, just because someone is writing numbers in the hotel, does that mean this is part of an organized crime operation? Chances are that it is. A person normally does not run a numbers bank on his own. He requires some backing and he must have sources to "lay off" some of his plays—i.e., he must get other bankers to take some of the betting action—to protect himself from a "big hit." The backing and these sources can only come from an organized business, the Cosa Nostra. There are very few, if any, large numbers banks today which are not part of the Cosa Nostra . . . and these operate only because they have been given a franchise to do so by the "Family" in control of the area.

Bookmaking

While numbers may not concern hotel management too much and they might overlook such activities (although we advise strongly that they do not take this attitude), bookmaking can also invade a hotel as easily as the numbers racket. Bookmaking, the taking of bets on horse races, can lead to greater problems since more money is involved. Numbers games can be run for pennies, dimes or any money value, while horse bets are usually at least two dollars. When someone feels he has a "hot tip," the wager can be considerable. The chances of winning on a horse are far greater than making a "hit" on the numbers, so more money is played.

Once again, what usually happens is that an employee is spending time on the job conducting a bookmaking business. The hotel loses not only the value of this employee, but also the time of each employee who stops and makes a bet. This lost time is serious enough from an efficiency standpoint, but the danger goes further. The horse player may develop other troubles which will affect his efficiency and pose a security problem for the hotel.

For example, John Doe is a houseman in a hotel but he is also a "numbers" runner and takes horse bets which he passes on to a bookie. In order to get around to all his customers in the hotel, he spends a good deal of his time making his rounds and calling in his bets. Bill Jones is a cook and he likes to play the horses. Bill has a few dollars in his pocket and last night he got a good "tip" down at the bowling alley. He contacts John Doe and places his bet, but unfortunately the horse does not win. The old determination to get even hits Bill and the following day he places another bet with John. Again, he has backed a loser. This may go on for a few days, weeks or months. Certainly Bill won't lose every bet, but in the long run he will be on the "short end." Sooner or later he will find that his finances are getting a little low. He has several choices at this stage: he can borrow money from fellow employees or other friends, or he can do a little stealing and go into business for himself. The thefts may be of hotel property, and this is where the danger lies.

We cannot control what a man does when he is off the job, but any form of gambling, whether it be craps, cards, horses or whatever, can have a serious effect on his efficiency and honesty while on the job. Just as a drug addict is forced to steal to support his habit (it has been estimated that an addict must steal $50,000 worth to get $10,000 in return; if his habit costs him $100 per day, this amount will only support him for 100 days), a gambler must steal or borrow to support his habit. Sooner or later he will run out of people to borrow from.

Drugs

Drugs probably create the most serious problems hotels face in connection with organized crime. Anyone who refuses to believe that organized crime is behind the drug market is very naive. It takes large sums of money to import drugs from foreign lands, and it takes many contacts and a complete organization to purchase, transport, and distribute the merchandise to the street peddlers. The tremendous amounts of money needed to support an addict create a strong motive for theft, so it is well for the security officer to be on the lookout for drug users. A great deal of help, not only in controlling the distribution of drugs but also in identifying possible users, can be obtained from various agencies responsible for the enforcement of drug laws.

Loan Sharking

The object of organized crime is to get the unsuspecting citizen involved in something that will become addictive to him, whether it be gambling, drugs, or whatever. "Get the sucker hooked and keep him on the line," is the philosophy of the Cosa Nostra. One of the most vicious businesses is that of the loan shark. A man in financial need borrows money from an organization banker. Such a transaction is very private and there are no questions asked; such would not be the case if the borrower were to go to a bank or other legitimate lending institution. For this privacy and immediate service, a high rate of interest is charged.

Unfortunately, the borrower soon finds it difficult to make his weekly payments and the interest charges pile up higher and higher. He may borrow additional money to make his payments due, but this merely compounds his problems. Soon he is faced with a situation where he is prone to blackmail, he is forced to steal or sell all he owns, or he may be the victim of violence. When a man finds himself in such a position, it is difficult to predict what he will do. He is concerned only with preserving his reputation, his life, his family at any cost, and if he must steal or commit fraud or betray confidences, he will do so. Again, it may well be the hotel which suffers from such actions.

Hijacking of Freight Transport

Hijacking and black market operations may also have an effect on a hotel. A truckload of meat or television sets is hijacked and is then offered to a prospective buyer at a price far below the current market price. The purchaser is unaware that the merchandise is stolen, as the offer to sell is based on the assumption that the seller just happened to come across a good deal and is able to offer the merchandise at a reduced rate. The story may be very convincing and the buyer may feel that he is getting a real bargain; however, anyone involved in purchasing should be very suspicious of strange suppliers offering bulk purchases at greatly reduced rates. We can only repeat what was said earlier: purchase only from known, reputable suppliers. It has been stated by law enforcement agencies and officers that if the "fences"—those who buy stolen property—could be put out of business, there would be no more stealing, since thieves would have no place to dispose of their loot. The average thief cannot simply go out on the street and peddle his wares without raising suspicion. He must work through a person or an organization that has some aura of respectability or many contacts. Again, organized crime has the facilities and the means of disposing of such bulk goods.

Prostitution

Prostitution is also in the repertoire of organized crime. Without commenting on the morality of such a business, we must abide by the law. If prostitution is illegal, the hotel should not risk its reputation and license by allowing such activities to go unchallenged.

Normally, for prostitution to function economically within a hotel, there must be an inside contact—a person or persons who can solicit business or who can fill requests when they are made by guests. Usually this has to be someone like the bellman or a room clerk, someone who is in contact with the guests at all times. This contact is actually an employee of the person operating the prostitution ring and is paid a commission for each arrangement or contract he delivers. This operation may be entirely unknown to management or may operate with management's knowledge.

The security officer should have a clear understanding with management as to the policy toward "organized prostitution" as opposed to the businessman who may "pick up" a companion outside the hotel and take her to his room, or the "cheater" who fraudulently registers with a woman claimed to be his wife. It is imperative that an organized prostitution operation within a hotel be avoided at all costs.

SUMMARY

The extent to which organized crime has infiltrated legitimate businesses or has affected such businesses is not fully known.

It was not until 1964, when Joseph Valachi, a high-ranking member of the Cosa Nostra, testified before a Congressional committee, that law enforcement agencies got their first real look into the operations of organized crime. Since that time, a great deal has been accomplished in uncovering these operations. However, many feel that the surface has merely been scratched and there is much more to be accomplished before the threat is eliminated.

As was pointed out earlier, many of organized crime's activities have gone "underground," so to speak, and a heavy layer of respectability has been applied as a cover. We can only suggest that a security officer be alert to any signs of gambling activity—numbers, horses, floating crap games, card games—within the hotel, whether indulged in by employees or guests, as well as signs of drug use or prostitution, and take whatever steps are necessary to put a stop to such activities.

The more a security officer knows about the subject, the better he will be able to detect suspicious activities. Advice and assistance can be secured from any law enforcement agency. If an officer desires a basic knowledge of what is involved in organized crime, we would recommend reading *The Valachi Papers*, by Peter Maas. There is no fiction in this book; rather it relates the facts as set forth by Valachi himself concerning the Cosa Nostra and organized crime.

Organized crime as embodied in the Cosa Nostra is certainly not responsible for all of the organized crime that takes place within this country or other English-speaking nations. Other groups do exist; however, most of these other groups rely more on active violence as opposed to the sly, undercover, non-violent type of crimes. If the hotel is owned by a parent company involved in some controversial industry, the hotel may be the target of violent demonstrations of disapproval. Hotels owned by foreign countries may be targets of dissenters, or government-owned hotels or buildings may be subjected to violent crimes. Such situations normally occur during worldwide crises, and the political climate within the nation must be considered by the security officer in his evaluation of the potential dangers to the property.

Chapter 18

Cooperating Agencies and Services Available

The job of maintaining security in a hotel cannot be accomplished by one man alone; it takes the combined efforts of many people. Managers and owners, as well as security officers, should realize that many organizations and agencies are ready and willing to assist if requested. There should be no hesitation on the part of a hotel or motel to ask for this assistance, as the advice and services offered may be just the answer to a given problem. Although we cannot cover here every possible source of assistance, we will attempt to list some of the most important.

HOTEL LAW

Comprehensive Book

Anyone interested in the history of hotel law, as well as a detailed and thorough examination of hotel law as it exists today, would be wise to secure a copy of *The Laws of Innkeepers, For Hotels, Motels, Restaurants, and Clubs,* by John H. Sherry, published by the Cornell University Press, 124 Roberts Place, Ithaca, New York 14850. Mr. Sherry has been a practicing attorney in New York City for a number of years and a Professor of Hotel Law at the Cornell University School of Hotel Administration. This book, the first comprehensive book on public hospitality law since 1906, is all-inclusive in its coverage of the applicable basic common law principles in every possible legal

211

situation. While the statutory coverage is limited to New York, the reader will find the information in this book not only useful but interesting regardless of where his property is located.

Laws Differ from Place to Place

Because of differing laws in various jurisdictions, specific questions pertaining to law in a given matter should be referred to competent legal counsel. Federal laws, formulated by Congress in the U.S. and by Parliament in Canada, include the Criminal Code as well as laws concerning drugs, customs, excise taxes and many other matters. Provincial or State laws, enacted by individual state or provincial legislatures, govern most hotel/motel operations. While these laws may be similar in broad terms, there are differences. In Canada, for example, there are ten different sets of laws, one for each province; in the United States, there are fifty sets, one for each state. Finally, there are municipal laws or ordinances passed by municipalities under authority granted them by the province or state. Naturally, these laws also vary from municipality to municipality, and what applies in one community may not apply in a neighboring town.

Hotel/Motel Associations

In many large urban areas, associations of hotel/motel operators exist as well as state or provincial associations. For example, there is an Atlantic City (New Jersey) Hotel/Motelman's Association, a New Jersey State Hotel/Motel Association, as well as the American Hotel/Motel Association. In Canada, as well as almost every other country, there is an association of hotelmen, dedicated to the advancement and development of the industry. These associations are normally well versed in the laws as they apply to the given area of jurisdiction. Many have legal counselors on their staffs, ready and willing to assist member hotels or motels. A great deal of help, advice and material can be secured from these associations.

BOARDS AND AGENCIES

While laws are passed on three different levels of government, the enforcement and application of such laws becomes the responsibility of numerous agencies, offices, commissions, and authorities. Just as the laws themselves differ, so do the names and titles of the administrators. For example, what is called the Liquor Control Board in Ontario, Canada, is known as the Alcoholic Beverage Control Commission in New Jersey, so our recommendations can only be made in general terms. In addition, we would suggest that initial inquiries be made at the local level. The local authorities can usually suggest the proper agency to handle the specific problem or request.

Alcoholic Beverages:
 Liquor Control Board
 Alcoholic Beverage Control Commission
 State Beverage Commission
Food and Food Products:
 Board of Health
 Federal Food and Drug Administration
Fire:
 Local Fire Department
 National Fire Protection Association, International
 Underwriters' Laboratories, Inc.
 Underwriters' Laboratories of Canada
 Fire Rating Bureau
 Underwriters' Association
 Board of Insurance Underwriters
 Fire Marshal's Office
 Insurance Companies
Criminal Activities:
 Local Police
 Sheriff
 State Highway Patrol
 R.C.M.P.
 F.B.I.
 Attorney General
Drugs:
 Any Police Agency
 Bureau of Narcotics and Dangerous Drugs
 Attorney General
Safety:
 Insurance Companies
 National Safety Council

Workman's Compensation Board or Commission
Labor Board
Department of Health, Education and Welfare
Department of Labor and Industry
Employee Relations:
Labor Relations Board
Applicable Union (if employees are members of union)
Department of Labor and Industry
Labor Board
Employee Benefits, etc.
Social Security Administration
Workman's Compensation Board
Department of Health, Education and Welfare
Labor Relations Board
Department of Labor and Industry
Trash, Garbage and Sanitation:
Board of Health
Department of Sanitation
Medical Association
Department of Public Works
Medical Facilities and Training:
Red Cross
Medical Association
Security Services or Equipment:
Usually such services are licensed by some regulatory agency such as the police. It would be well to check with the police to determine credibility or legitimacy, or with the Better Business Bureau, Consumers Protective Association, or local, state or national organizations such as the Security Equipment Industry Association, Locksmiths Institute, etc.

SOURCES OF SECURITY INFORMATION

Security Associations

In many areas local associations of security officers have been formed in an attempt to foster better relations, education and social occasions among members of the same profession. Membership in such a group is often beneficial. Many times helpful information can be exchanged at meetings where local conditions are discussed and joint action can be taken. In addition, there are publications dealing with all phases of security which are well worth the price. These materials include magazines, books and pamphlets, as well as audio tape cassettes.

Seminars

One of the newest contributions to the security industry has been the availability of a number of seminars offered throughout the country. In many cases, these meetings include sessions dealing specifically with all phases of hotel and restaurant security. A careful review of programs offered will often reveal a worthwhile seminar where hotel security officers and/or managers can hear and talk with top experts in the field. Membership or attendance in any group, association or meeting should not be considered merely for the sake of belonging, but rather should be undertaken only if the participant intends to become a contributing part of that group to improve his own knowledge and perhaps help his fellow security-minded associates.

Information on Criminals

Membership in some professional hotel organizations entitles the members to periodic bulletins listing persons wanted for crimes against member hotels or warning against such persons. In the case of the American Hotel/Motel Association, this bulletin is prepared by the Burns International Detective Agency and is complete with photographs and biographies of those wanted or warned against. In some cases, rewards are offered for information leading to the arrest of such persons. If such bulletins are received, they should be carefully read by the security officer, given wide distribution to hotel cashiers, clerks, and credit managers, and retained for ready reference.

Security Education

Community colleges in many areas are now offering courses in career-type subjects leading to associate degrees. Such educational opportunities should not be overlooked by either the new or the experienced security officer. While such courses may be in industrial security rather than limited to hotel security, much good can be gained by this study. The furthering of one's education in professional subjects and in the arts must have a beneficial result in one's development. Today's leader, whether a businessman, a security officer, a police officer, or a member of any other profession, must be knowledgeable not only about his own field but about life in general. The educational opportunities available in many areas today make such knowledge readily available to all interested persons. The security industry as a whole is one of the largest and fastest-growing industries in the world today and there is going to be a great demand for trained, educated leaders. The law enforcement and security officers of today are a new breed, and it is education that has made and will make the difference in success or failure of the individual.

One of the authors of this book attended the Hotel Administration School at Cornell University during the late 1940's. In four years of study, the subject of hotel security was never discussed aside from instruction in hotel law. What was learned in the following years was learned by experience (sometimes very costly) "on the job." To our knowledge, this is one of the first books ever published dealing with the specific problems connected with hotel security. It is only a starting point, an attempt to generate thinking so that new systems and new procedures may be developed to improve hotel/motel security.

The Future

What is the future of hotel security? Two of the major concerns of the hotel industry today are rapidly rising costs and an escalating crime rate. The consumer is being "ripped off" twice . . . first in the cost of items stolen and secondly in the cost of security measures.

Security must therefore be truly cost-effective, and every security dollar must be made to count. This can only happen as the result of constant security education. To this end we respectfully submit this book.

Appendix A

United States Laws Relating to Hotels and Motels

There are many statutes, both Federal and State, which affect the hotel/motel industry in the U.S. to some degree. While the Federal Law takes precedence and applies throughout the land, each State has laws which apply to that State. There are, therefore, fifty sets of State laws which, while similar in content, may differ in title, language and application. Since it would be impractical to cover all fifty states here, this appendix will set forth certain laws of the State of New Jersey as an example. The reader should check the laws that apply in his own State for specific information.

FEDERAL

Under Federal Law, those applying most directly to hotels include:
The Criminal Code
The Federal Food and Drug Act
The Federal Unemployment Insurance Act
The Federal Occupational Safety and Health Act

STATE OF NEW JERSEY

Most of the laws relating to hotels are found in the publications referred to as New Jersey Statutes Annotated (NJSA) under specific titles. The titles most applicable in the operation and management of a hotel or motel would be the following:

2A   Administration of Civil and Criminal Justice
10   Civil Rights
24   Food and Drugs
29   Hotels
33   Intoxicating Liquors
34   Labor and Workman's Compensation

NJSA Title 2A — Administration of Civil and Criminal Justice

Chapter 108 — Food and Drugs
Sect. 1 — Prohibits the sale of unwholesome food, drink or liquor; describes same, and sets forth penalties for violations.
Sect. 4 — Prohibits the mislabeling or the use of misleading advertising in the sale or offering of oleo which might lead the consumer to believe he is buying or consuming butter. Sets forth penalties for violations.
Sect. 5 — Prohibits use of labels or advertising that might lead to assumption that certain nonkosher foods were kosher.
Sect. 7 — Sets forth penalties for violation of Sect. 5.

Chapter 111 — Frauds and Cheats
Sect. 16 — Indicates that a bad check offered with the knowledge that insufficient funds exist to cover same, is prima facie evidence of intent to defraud.
Sect. 19 — Defrauding Hotels — This section in its entirety is usually printed and placed in each bedroom of a hotel or motel.

"Any person who obtains credit or accommodations at any hotel, inn, boarding house or lodging house, by means of any false pretense, or who with intent to defraud the proprietor thereof, or his agent or servant obtains any credit or accommodation at such place without paying therefor is guilty of a misdemeanor.

"Proof that lodging, food or other accommodation was obtained by false or fictitious showing, or pretense of baggage, or that the person refused or neglected to pay for such food, lodging or other accommodation upon demand, or removed or caused to be removed his baggage without paying for such food, lodging or other accommodation is presumptive evidence of fraudulent intent, but this section shall not apply where there has been a special agreement for delay in payment."

Sect. 42 — Defines a stolen credit card and sets forth penalties for possession or use of same.
Sect. 43-44 — Sets forth penalties for use of stolen credit card with intent to defraud and provides further for the penalties to those who know a credit card to be stolen and who issue money or other things of value regardless of this knowledge.

NJSA Title 10 — Civil Rights

Chapter 1 — Sect. 2 — Ensures equal rights and privileges of all persons in public places.
Sect. 5 — Defines public places to include "inn, tavern, road

house or hotel, whether for entertainment of transient guests or accommodation of those seeking health, recreation or rest; any restaurant, eating house or place where food is sold for consumption on the premises. . . . "

Sect. 6 – Sets forth penalties for violation of previous sections.

NJSA Title 24 – Food and Drug

Chapter 3 – Sect. 1 – Establishes Board of Health and gives authority to State Board or Local Board of Health to enter premise to inspect.

Sect. 2-4 – Gives right of Board of Health representative to take samples for analysis with or without owner's consent.

Chapter 14 – Oysters, Clams and Other Shellfish
Sect. 7 – Gives right to Board of Health to inspect.
Sect. 4 – Evidence accepted indicating food used for human consumption.

Chapter 15 – Sanitation
Sect. 1 – Defines food establishment which includes "Hotel" and "Restaurant." Covers requirements of construction, lighting, ventilation, cleanliness, protection from contamination, clothing of employees, toilet facilities, removal of refuse, and provisions for time to correct violations rather than face prosecution.
Chapter 17 – Provides for penalties for violations of Health Code.

Sub-Title 2 of Title 24 – Narcotic Drugs

Chapter 18 – Uniform Narcotic Drug Law – States that no one is allowed to have narcotic drugs in his possession without a prescription from a doctor.
Sect. 37 – Prohibits the use of a building for the purpose of using drugs. Provides that a building so used shall be considered a public nuisance and the authorities may act accordingly.

NJSA Title 29 – Hotels

Chapter 1 – Hotel Fire Protection
Sect. 1 – Sets forth specifications as apply to construction to provide for safety of guests in the event of fire and means of escape.
Sect. 8-9 – Establishes authority and duty to carry out provisions

of Act. Provides for Supervisor of Hotel Fire Safety in State Department of Law.

Sect. 11-19 — Defines "Hotel" and "Mixed Occupancy" as applied to this Act as well as "Guest Room," "Existing Hotel," "Basement," "Curb," and various types of construction allowed.

Sect. 20 — Requirements and specifications for fire escapes.

Sect. 22-23 — Requirements for exits, halls and passages and need for floor plan showing nearest exit to be placed in every bedroom.

Sect. 24-26 — Sets forth requirements for fire extinguishers, alarm systems, detection systems, and/or patrols.

Sect. 36 — Sets forth requirements for registration, inspection and registration fees to be charged.

Sect. 42 — Penalties for violators.

Chapter 2 — Liability to Guests

Sect. 1 — Defines "Hotel" and "Guest" for purpose of Act.

Sect. 2 — This is one of the three sections that is normally posted in each guest room to limit the liability of the innkeeper for valuables. It is reproduced in full as follows:

"Liability For Valuables. Whenever the proprietor of any hotel shall provide a safe or other depository in the office thereof, or other convenient place for the safekeeping of any money, jewels, furs, bank notes, precious stones, railroad tickets, ornaments or negotiable or valuable papers belonging to guests in such hotel, and shall place in a conspicuous position in the room or rooms occupied by such guests, a notice stating the fact that such safe or depository is provided in which money, jewels, furs, bank notes, precious stones, railroad tickets, ornaments or negotiable or valuable papers may be deposited, and guest shall neglect to deliver such money, jewels, furs, bank notes, precious stones, railroad tickets, ornaments or negotiable or valuable papers to the person in charge of such safe or depository, the proprietor of such hotel shall not be liable in any sum for the loss of such property sustained by such guest, by theft or otherwise. If such guest shall deliver such property to the person in charge of the office of such hotel for deposit in such safe or other depository, such hotel proprietor shall not be liable for any loss thereof sustained by such guest, by theft or otherwise, in any sum exceeding five hundred ($500.00) dollars unless by special agreement in writing with such proprietor or his duly authorized agent."

Sect. 3 — Liability for Property Other Than Valuables. This is the second of three notices normally posted in each guest room and reads in full as follows:

"No proprietor of any hotel, apartment house, inn or boarding house shall be liable in any sum to any guest, tenant, boarder or lodger for the loss of wearing apparel, goods, merchandise or other property, unless it shall appear that such loss occurred through the fault or negligence of such proprietor, nor shall any such proprietor be liable for any sum for the loss of any article or articles of wearing apparel, trunk, satchel, valise, bag, box, bundle, or the contents thereof, or any property belonging to any such guest, tenant, boarder, or lodger in any hotel, apartment hotel, inn or boarding house, and not within a room or rooms assigned to him unless that same shall be especially entrusted to the care and custody of such proprietor or his duly authorized agent, and if so especially entrusted with such article or articles of wearing apparel, trunk, satchel, valise, bag, box and bundle and the contents thereof, or any other property belonging to such guest, or traveler, the proprietor shall not be liable for the loss of same in any sum exceeding one hundred dollars ($100.00)."

Sect. 4 — Liability for Loss by Fire or Force. This is the third section normally found printed and placed in each guest bedroom and reads in full as follows:

"The proprietor of any hotel shall be liable to any guest in such hotel only for ordinary and reasonable care in the custody of any money, jewels, furs, bank notes, precious stones, railroad tickets, ornaments, negotiable or valuable papers, baggage, wearing apparel or other chattel, or property belonging to any such guest, whether specially entrusted to such proprietor or his agent or deposited in the safe or other depository of such hotel or otherwise, for any loss occasioned by fire or by any other force over which such proprietor has no control."

NJSA Title 33 — Intoxicating Liquors

Chapter 1, Sect. 3 — Sets up Department of Alcoholic Beverage Control and sets forth duties of same.

Sect. 9-22 — Sets forth types of licenses to be issued, issuing authority, number to be issued, fees, renewals, transfers, etc. For example, a Class C License is defined as follows:

"Holder may sell, subject to rules and regulations, for consumption on licensed premises, any alcoholic beverage by the glass or other receptacle, and also may sell all alcoholic beverage in original containers for consumption off the licensed premises."

Sect. 25-27 — Application requirements, fees and terms of licenses are set forth.

Sect. 31 — Outlines grounds for revocation of license.
1. Violation of any provisions of Act or
2. Violation of any rules and regulations promulgated by Commissioner of Alcoholic Beverage Commission.

Sect. 35 — Gives right and authority to investigate, inspect, search and examine premises and materials contained thereon.

Sect. 39 — Gives authority to Commissioner of Alcoholic Beverage Control Commission to make such general rules and regulations as may be necessary for proper regulation and control of the manufacture, sales and distribution of alcoholic beverage and the enforcement of the Act, including hours of sale.

The Rules and Regulations, published as such by the Commissioner, are all-inclusive, covering every aspect of manufacture, sale and service of alcoholic beverages. As they apply to hotels, such matters as offering free drinks, advertising, hours of operation, conduct of patrons, provisions for rest rooms, persons to be employed in the handling, selling or servicing, requirements for registration of out-of-state employees, registration of aliens, reports, etc., are all covered. These rules and regulations must be adhered to without fail; violators are subject to strict penalties.

NJSA Title 34 — Workman's Compensation

This title covers all the aspects of the Workman's Compensation Law as it applies almost universally throughout the United States. Everything having to do with the health and welfare of employees is covered in this Act and should be reviewed carefully by each security officer.

Appendix B

Canadian Laws Relating to Hotels and Motels

There are many statutes, both Federal and Provincial, which to some degree affect the hotel industry in Canada. This appendix is intended to direct the reader's attention to those which most directly relate to hotels and motels and therefore should be familiar to those in positions of responsibility.

For a detailed description of each statute, reference must be made to up-to-date copies of the actual statutes. These are available in libraries or law offices, and it is pointless to cover them in full detail here. Only the most frequently required statutes are described briefly in this appendix.

The Federal laws apply in all of Canada, but Provincial law applies only in the particular province. It follows, therefore, that to cover Provincial law completely, ten sets of statutes would have to be included. This would be unwieldy, and therefore only the statutes applying to Ontario are included. The laws of the other provinces are similar in broad terms, but differ in detail. The reader in another province, therefore, can use the Ontario listings as a guide to find legislation on similar subject areas in his particular area.

Brief remarks follow in reference to the statutes listed below.

FEDERAL

The Criminal Code (certain sections), RSC 1970 Chapter C-34
The Food and Drug Act, RSC 1970 Chapter F-27
The Tobacco Restraint Act, RSC 1970 Chapter T-9
The Unemployment Insurance Act, RSC 1970 Chapter U-2

PROVINCIAL

The Innkeepers Act (RSO 1970 Chapter 223)
The Hotel Registration of Guests Act (RSO 1970 Chapter 212)

The Petty Trespass Act (RSO 1970 Chapter 347)
The Liquor License Act 1975 (Ontario Statutes 1975 Chapter 40)
The Oleomargarine Act (RSO 1970 Chapter 304)
The Hotel Fire Safety Act (Ontario Statutes 1971 Chapter 41)
The Municipal Act (RSO 1970 Chapter 284)
The Tourism Act (RSO 1970 Chapter 122)
The Elevators and Lifts Act (RSO 1970 Chapter 143)
The Industrial Safety Act (Ontario Statutes 1971 Chapter 43)
Labour Relations Act (RSO 1970 Chapter 232)
The One Day's Rest in Seven Act (RSO 1970 Chapter 305)
The Public Health Act (RSO 1970 Chapter 377)
The Workmen's Compensation Act (RSO 1970 Chapter 505)

FEDERAL STATUTES

The Criminal Code, RSC 1970 Chapter C-34

The following sections may affect hotel premises to some extent and are shown as reference only. For detail, the actual sections should be studied.

Sect. 185 – Keeping a gaming or betting house.
Sect. 186 – Allowing premises to be used for registering bets.
Sect. 192 – Cheating at play.
Sect. 193 – Keeping a bawdy house.
Sect. 195.1 – Soliciting prostitution.
Sect. 294 – Theft.
Sect. 302 – Robbery.
Sect. 306 – Breaking and entering with intent.
Sect. 312 – Possession of property obtained in Canada by an indictable offense.
Sect. 320 – Obtaining by means of a false pretense.
Sect. 322 – Fraudulently obtaining food and lodging.
Sect. 338 – Fraud.

The Food and Drug Act, RSC 1970 Chapter F-27

There are two statutes which directly affect the food service operation in a hotel. The first one is the Food and Drug Act, which is a federal statute, and the second is the Oleomargarine Act of Ontario. (The Ontario act will be discussed later under Provincial statutes.)

The Food and Drug Act covers many subject areas, including food, drugs, cosmetics and devices, the latter term being used in regard to certain equipment of a medical nature. The main purpose of the statute is to protect the public from adulterated products and to control or prohibit the use of certain drugs. It is in this latter area that the statute is best known to the public on account of the prevalent use of the amphetamines, commonly known as "speed," and also the hallucinogens, an example of which is LSD. These areas should not be of concern to hotel managers, unless persons involved in "pushing" these drugs attempt to make sales on hotel premises, and if they are detected so doing, the police should be called immediately. It is also to be hoped that no hotel employee will use any of these drugs.

The Food and Drug Act consists of the following:

1. Part I — Food, Drugs, Cosmetics and Devices.
2. Part II — Administration and Enforcement.
3. Part III — Controlled Drugs.
4. Part IV — Restricted Drugs.
5. Eight Schedules — A to H.

There are also voluminous Regulations made pursuant to the Act. These are frequently changing. We will only concern ourselves with the food area which is covered in Parts I and II. The Regulations are also of concern, but they require reading in detail and are too lengthy to be discussed here. The Act is administered by the Federal Department of Consumer and Corporate Affairs, any member of which may be designated as an inspector by the Governor in Council pursuant to Section 25 of the Act. The more important sections from a hotel point of view include the following:

Sect. 2 — Contains several definitions including "food," which means any food, drink or ingredient for human consumption including chewing gum.
Sect. 4 — Prohibits any sale of food that is in any way impure or adulterated or prepared under unsanitary conditions. This point is of importance in respect to hotel kitchens and food storage areas. These are open to inspection by designated inspectors.
Sect. 5, 6, 7 — Prohibits sale of food in misleading packages, provides for standards in packaging and prohibits storage under unsanitary conditions.
Sect. 8-21 — These deal with drugs, cosmetics and devices and will not be commented on here.
Sect. 22 — Part II of the Act commences here and this section deals with the powers of inspectors, which include power to:

1. Enter any premises at a reasonable time without warrant. This infers when the premises are open for business.

2. Open receptacles and packages on such premises.
3. Examine books and documents.
4. Seize any article which may be evidence of an offense under the Act.

Inspectors are given certificates of identity which they must produce on request. Persons in charge of premises are to assist the inspector as far as possible. Obstruction or the making of false statements are offenses.

Sect. 23 — Provides for seized articles to be returned to the owner if they comply with the Act or Regulations, and also provides for forfeiture and/or destruction which may be by owner's consent or by court order.

Sect. 24 — Empowers an inspector to submit any seized article for analysis or examination.

Sect. 25 — Empowers the Governor in Council to make regulations under the Act respecting several subject areas, the most important from a hotel point of view being the following:

1. Declaration of food as adulterated.
2. Use of ingredients.
3. Setting standards.
4. Preventing consumers being defrauded.
5. Appointment and powers of inspectors.
6. Storage, etc., of food and drugs.

Sect. 26 — This covers offenses and penalties, which are quite severe. On summary conviction, a fine of $500.00 and/or sentence of up to three months for a first offense; $1,000.00 and/or six months for subsequent offenses; a fine of up to $5,000.00 and/or up to three years' imprisonment when convicted on indictment. Any contravention of the Act or Regulations constitutes an offense. The severity of the penalties is intended to provide a deterrent for the protection of the public in this most important area.

Sect. 27 — Time limit for prosecutions is 12 months after the time the offense was committed.

Sect. 28-32 — These conclude Part II and contain miscellaneous provisions including evidentiary matters. They are not particularly important except to an accused person. One interesting point to note is that, if an offense is committed by an employee or agent of the accused, the accused will be liable to conviction under the provisions of Section 31 (2). Also under Section 31 (4), where a person is prosecuted in respect of adulterated food, the onus of proving that the food was not adulterated lies on the accused rather than the Crown having to prove adulteration.

This concludes the provisions of the Food and Drug Act as they apply to hotel managers. It should be noted that the powers outlined in Section 22 apply only to inspectors, not the police. However, the police do enforce the provisions of Parts III and IV dealing with controlled restricted drugs.

The Tobacco Restraint Act, RSC 1970 Chapter T-9

The purpose of this short statute is to prevent, as far as possible, persons apparently under the age of 16 from possessing and using tobacco products. It should be enforced more than it is.

> *Sect. 2* — Sales, direct or indirect, constitute an offense by both seller and buyer.
>
> *Sect. 3* — Tobacco products found in possession of persons apparently under 16 may be seized by a constable or by a law enforcement officer.
>
> *Sect. 4* — Person apparently under 16 smoking—penalty from $1.00 to $4.00.
>
> *Sect. 5* — Of interest to hotel keepers, as an offense is created where persons under 16 are habitually using a vending machine. This may result in a court order to remove the machine with a fine of $5.00 for every day following that the order is not complied with.

The Unemployment Insurance Act, RSC 1970 Chapter U-2

This statute will apply to every full-time employee in a hotel and requires employer and employee to contribute to unemployment insurance. The Statute is quite long and detailed. Assistance in its application can be obtained from offices of the Unemployment Insurance Commission or a Canada Manpower Centre.

PROVINCIAL STATUTES

The Innkeepers Act, RSO 1970 Chapter 223

> *Sect. 1* — An inn and innkeeper are both defined. This includes a hotel, inn, tavern, public house or other place of refreshment, the

keeper of which is responsible by law for the goods of the guests.
Sect. 2 — Provides some protection of the innkeeper by giving
him a lien on the goods of guests in respect to the cost of food
and lodging provided. The section explains how the innkeeper
may sell such goods at public auction to settle unpaid accounts.
The section is probably difficult to invoke in practice because the
guest may either take his goods when he leaves or perhaps have
no goods of any value.
Sect. 3 — Makes similar provision in respect of horses and
carriages in regard to caring for them in livery stables. The
provisions cannot be invoked in respect to automobiles.
Sect. 4 — An important one because it covers liabilities:

1. An innkeeper is liable for the property of his guests up
   to the sum of $40.00, except for horses and carriages.
2. He is liable for the full value if over $40.00 if the goods
   were deposited for safekeeping, or if the loss was caused
   by negligence or willful acts of employees, or if he fails
   to display the notice required by Section 6.

Sect. 5 — If the innkeeper refuses to accept for safekeeping any
property which a guest wishes to deposit with him, he loses the
protection of Section 4 limiting his liability.
Sect. 6 — The innkeeper is required to display prominently a
copy of Section 4 in all public rooms and every bedroom. If he
fails to do so, he will lose the protection of Section 4 and is fully
liable for any losses incurred by guests. It appears that this
section is more honored in the non-observance than otherwise,
and hotel managers would be wise to follow its provisions.
Sect. 7 — This section contains general provisions pursuant to the
foregoing in respect to court orders and sale of guests' property.
The most important provisions are that after sale of the guest's
property, any sum that is in excess of the account outstanding
shall be returned to the guest, and also that the guest, before sale,
may settle his account and get his property back unless a
magistrate orders otherwise. Any contravention of these provisions may be punished by a fine of up to $50.00 or imprisonment
up to 30 days.

This completes the provisions of the Innkeepers Act and also clearly
demonstrates the requirement for security measures to be in effect at hotels
so that this statute may be properly complied with.

The Hotel Registration of Guests Act, RSO 1970 Chapter 212

Sect. 1 — Defines a hotel for the purpose of the statute. This includes hotels with the exception of:

1. Boarding or lodging houses which let rooms by the week or more.
2. Those with less than six guest bedrooms.
3. Those premises classed as "apartment houses" or "private hotels."

Sect. 2 — This contains the main requirement of the Act, which is that every person to whom accommodation is provided shall register by recording his correct name and usual place of residence. This applies to all persons given accommodation, not merely the payer. For example, every member of a family should be registered, not just the father. Most registration forms also provide for recording the make and license number of guests' cars. This is not required by the Act, and guests cannot legally be forced to disclose this information, but it is a wise security measure against fraud, and potential guests can always be refused accommodation if they refuse to comply. However, this will usually be difficult to enforce.

Sect. 3 — Provides a penalty of not less than $10.00 or more than $50.00 or imprisonment in default of payment in respect of:

1. A manager who fails to keep a register.
2. A manager who permits false registration.

Sect. 4 — Provides for offenses by guests which carry a fine of not less than $20.00 or more than $200.00 or imprisonment in default in respect of:

1. Registering in a false name.
2. Registering a false address.

This section cannot be invoked against a guest who gives false automobile information.

Sect. 5 — Requires the manager to post a notice in every bedroom indicating the rates charged for that room. Penalty for non-compliance is a fine of up to $100.00.

The strange thing about this statute is that it does not empower the police to inspect hotel registers on demand, but the practice is to allow this to be done when so requested by the police, and this is as it should be. It is most important for hotel managers to maintain good liaison and cooperation with the local police because there are areas where police assistance can be very useful. This should be obvious without further elaboration.

The Petty Trespass Act, RSO 1970 Chapter 347

Before getting into the provisions of this statute, we must define a trespasser, who may be either:

1. A person who enters the land or property of another without authority or consent and against the wishes of the owner, or
2. A person who, having entered with consent, refuses to leave when the consent is withdrawn.

The public has an implied right of access to hotel premises, and the operative word is "implied." This means that right of access is conditional on the assumption that entrance is for a lawful and reasonable purpose, and therefore the right of access may be withdrawn by the owner or his authorized agent at any time and no reason has to be stated for such withdrawal. This is the basis of the Petty Trespass Act. Its provisions are as follows:

> *Sect. 1* — Every person who trespasses on the land of another that is enclosed, or a garden or lawn, or warned not to trespass by sign or verbally, commits an offense and is liable to a fine of from $10.00 to $100.00. This also applies to motor vehicles, and the owner of the vehicle is liable as well as the driver if the vehicle was under his control.
>
> *Sect. 2* — Trespassers may be arrested without warrant by a peace officer, the owner of the property or his authorized agent.
>
> *Sect. 3* — Persons may not be charged with an offense under this Act where there is a disputed claim to the title of the land.
>
> *Sect. 4* — Precludes conviction for trespass where the accused satisfies the court that he had a reasonable belief that he was entitled to do the act complained of, and also if he is charged with the offense of willfully causing damage under the value of $50.00 (Section 388 of the Criminal Code).

The Liquor License Act 1975

This Act, together with the Liquor Control Act of 1975, regulates and controls the sale and consumption of alcoholic beverages in Ontario. Similar legislation exists in all provinces of Canada. The main purpose is to ensure that sales remain a government monopoly to secure provincial revenue. The Liquor Control Act consists of eleven sections and is not of interest to hotels. It describes the composition and marketing functions of the Liquor Control Board of Ontario and contains no regulatory matter requiring enforcement.

Sect. 1 – Contains some basic definitions relating to alcoholic products. This Act also contains all the enforcement provisions.

Sect. 2-3 – Terms of reference and composition of the Liquor License Board, which consists of seven members.

Sect. 4 – Contains the offense of selling without a license in Subsection (1). Offenses mentioned in various sections of the Act all come within the scope of Sect. 54, which is the punishment section. Sect. 4 also allows transfer and temporary transfer of licenses.

Sect. 5-7 – Deal generally with licenses, and the following should be noted:

   a. Sect. 6 outlines class of persons to whom a license will not be given, including: Non-Canadians or landed immigrants; financially unstable persons or firms; unsuitable premises of applicant; manufacturer's agents.
   b. Under Sect. 7, licenses last for two years and are renewable on application.

Sect. 8 – Special occasion permits. These are normally issued for special occasions, to permit supply on non-licensed premises for affairs such as wedding receptions, etc.

Sect. 9-21 – Further details *re* licenses and permits. The decisions of the Liquor License Board may be appealed to the Liquor License Appeal Tribunal (Sect. 13-14), but the decisions of the tribunal are final (Sect. 18).

Sect. 22 – Investigations by the Liquor License Board. This section should be noted, as it contains the offense of obstructing the investigation and makes provision for the issuance of a search warrant for investigative purposes which police must execute if requested. Necessary force may be used in the search, and evidence of offenses against this Act may be seized. Warrants to be executed by day unless specially endorsed by the issuing provincial judge. A justice is not authorized to issue this warrant. Note that documents may only be removed for copying purposes and are then to be returned.

   These investigations may be ordered by the Liquor License Board on a reasonable belief that offenses against this Act or the regulations are occurring, or that Criminal Code or other statute offenses have occurred affecting the person's fitness to hold a license.

Sect. 23 — Inspectors. These are designated by the Board in writing and may enter licensed premises to check observance of the Act. Obstructing these persons is an offense.

Sect. 24 — Inspection of licensed manufacturers. Not relevant to hotels.

Sect. 25 — Investigation and inspection results to be kept confidential.

Sect. 26-34 — The taking of liquor votes. Not relevant to hotels.

Sect. 35 — Interdiction orders. These may be appealed as for a license. Possession of liquor while interdicted is an offense, and persons subject to these orders must deliver all stocks of liquor to the Board. The liquor will be returned when the order is revoked. In practice it is more likely that the Board would buy the liquor from the interdicted person and the section allows for this. Selling or supplying to interdicted persons is an offense.

Sect. 36 — Revocation of interdiction orders. Not relevant to hotels.

Sect. 37-38 — Detoxification centers for the treatment of alcoholism. Where police find a person intoxicated under Sect. 46, they may take him to a center as an alternative to laying a charge. The staff of these centers are protected against damage suits relevant to treatment procedures. Under Sect. 38, provincial judges may make an order for detention in a detoxification center for up to 90 days.

Sect. 39 — Licensing of manufacturer's agents. Not relevant to hotels.

Sect. 40 — Power to make regulations. Included is the power to prescribe types of license. These include:

Lounge License — any liquor.

Dining Lounge License — any liquor with meals.

Dining Room License — beer or wine with meals.

Entertainment Lounge License — liquor with live entertainment.

Public House License — beer only.

Club License — any liquor.

Club License Restricted — beer or wine with food. Beer without.

Patio License — liquor out-of-doors.

Hospitality License — liquor without charge.

Manufacturer's License — for manufacture of liquor.

Pursuant to this, Regulation No. 1008/75 has been promulgated. It should be studied, as it contains many matters which concern licenses.

Sect. 41 — Definition of liquor. The next 13 sections deal with enforcement and offenses.

Sect. 42 — Purchase only from authorized outlets.

Sect. 43 — Prohibits manufacturers from donating liquor. This was a common practice to boost sales at one time.

Sect. 44 — No sale to drunken persons.

Sect. 45 — Under 18 years:

    a. No sales to such persons.
    b. Sellers or suppliers and receivers all commit offenses.
    c. Judge may determine age from appearance.
    d. Persons under 18 only permitted in certain types of licensed premises.
    e. Parents may supply minors in a residence.
    f. Liquor identity cards available from Liquor Control Board of Ontario.

Sect. 46 — "Public place" and "residence" defined.

    a. Consumption only in licensed premises or a residence.
    b. No public intoxication. Power of arrest for this where necessary to protect from injury.

Sect. 47 — Power of license to evict undesirables.

Sect. 48 — Liquor may not be kept in vehicles unless:

    a. Seal unbroken.
    b. Packed so as not to be accessible, if seal unbroken.

Conveyances and persons may be searched by police without warrant.

Sect. 49 — Offense to drink, or supply for drinking, alcohol that is not intended for human consumption (e.g., hair tonic).

Sect. 50 — No advertising of liquor except as in regulations.

Sect. 51 — Sales other than via an authorized outlet will cause liquor to be forfeited to Liquor Control Board of Ontario.

Sect. 52 — Liquor identity cards.

Sect. 53 — Civil liability against people who sell liquor to intoxicated persons, thereby giving rise to possible death or injury or damage to property. An important section for licenses.

Sect. 54 — Punishment section for all offenses. Maximum penalty for persons is $2,000 fine or one year imprisonment. For a corporation, $25,000.

Sect. 55 — Evidence of any statement by the Board.

Sect. 56 — Certificates cannot be challenged.

Sect. 57 — Exception for drugs.

Sect. 58-60 — Transitional.

The foregoing has been a very brief outline of the main highlights of the Liquor License Act 1975, and the intention of this review has not been to impart a working knowledge of these statutes. However, it is hoped that sufficient information has been included to convince those involved in the hotel trade that it is essential to acquire at least a fair idea of their provisions.

The Oleomargarine Act, RSO 1970 Chapter 304

This is the other statute affecting food services in a hotel. Perhaps these days it is somewhat outmoded, but as it applies to hotels (among other business premises), hotel managers should at least be aware of it. The purpose of the statute is to prevent the public being fraudulently deceived by persons attempting to represent margarine as butter. As is well known, the two substances are similar in appearance, but butter is considerably more expensive than margarine. There is, of course, no objection to persons being given or sold margarine as long as they are clearly informed that it is margarine they are getting. The statute was introduced many years ago at the request of the dairy industry to protect themselves against the inroads being made into the butter market by margarine interests. The statute has application in any premises where the public may be given or sold margarine and includes hotels and other places of refreshment.

Sect. 2 — Requires such premises which serve margarine to include on the menu the words "Oleomargarine is served here." Where no menu is used, these words will be displayed on a prominent sign.

Sect. 3 — The mixing of oleomargarine and butter for sale in eating places is forbidden.

Sect. 4 — Controls the coloring of margarine.

Sect. 5-6 — Control misleading packaging and forbid manufacture without a license.

Sect. 6a-6g — Particulars re licenses.

Sect. 7 — Controls misleading advertising and forbids any pictorial representation depicting any form of dairy scene connected with oleomargarine.

Sect. 8 — Empowers the Lieutenant Governor to appoint inspectors to enforce the Act.

Sect. 9 — Empowers the Lieutenant Governor to make regulations controlling standards, manufacture, inspectors, etc.

Sect. 10 — Penalties for contravention—on summary conviction, a fine up to $500.00 and/or imprisonment for up to 6 months.

The Hotel Fire Safety Act, Ontario Statutes 1970 Chapter 41

This Act is one of the statutes which deal with fire safety in hotels. It is an Ontario statute, as is the other relevant one, the Municipal Act. The purpose of the Hotel Fire Safety Act is to stipulate construction specifications for various types of hotels to ensure protection to occupants in the event of fire and provide means of escape. The main concern of the manager must be to ensure that his premises complies with the various specifications, because he will get into serious trouble if it does not. The statute as amended should be in possession of all hotel managers because of the detailed specifications contained therein, and there is no point in detailing all of them here. Some of the interesting points include:

Sect. 1 — Contains definitions, among which are:

1. "Hotel" is interpreted as an establishment providing sleeping accommodation and is licensed under the Liquor License Act and the Tourism Act.
2. "Inspector" is a person designated by the Lieutenant Governor to enforce this Act. They conduct periodic inspections of hotels to ensure compliance.

Sect. 2-9 — These contain design and building specifications and means of escape from fire.

Sect. 10 — Particulars relating to "Exit" notices.

Sect. 11-14 — Further specifications and instructions regarding sprinklers or watchmen.

Sect. 17 — An important one. Failure to comply with the specifications constitutes an offense punishable by a fine of up to $1,000.00 and the magistrate may, on conviction, order closure. Also a conviction is no bar to further prosecution. This means that if the accused is convicted for non-compliance with the Act, failure to correct the situation can result in further charges.

Sect. 19 — Empowers the Lieutenant Governor to make regulations. These include the requirement to submit plans of proposed new construction or alterations to the Fire Marshal of Ontario for approval.

Sect. 20 — Nothing in this Act affects the validity of municipal by-laws where such enforce more stringent standards of fire safety. This point will be further discussed under the Municipal Act.

The Municipal Act, RSO 1970 Chapter 284

This statute, which is very long and complex, affects hotels in regard to several areas, among them fire safety. The purpose of the statute is to control and regulate the government of a municipality, as no municipality can pass by-laws except on subjects authorized by the Municipal Act. There are two paragraphs which affect fire safety in hotels, as follows:

Sect. 354 (1) para. 27 — This empowers the municipality to make by-laws "for securing against accident by fire the inmates and employees and others in . . . hotels . . . etc."
Sect. 354 (1) para. 44 — The municipality may make by-laws for "making such other regulations for preventing fires as council may deem necessary."

The second paragraph is not, of course, confined to hotels. The effect of this is that any municipality may create legislation binding on hotels located within that municipality, in respect to fire safety. Therefore hotel managers must ascertain what by-laws may be in effect in their respective locations in addition to the requirements of the Hotel Fire Safety Act. However, a by-law which had the effect of relaxing any requirement of the Hotel Fire Safety Act would be invalid.

There are other areas of hotel operations which may be affected by municipal by-laws apart from fire safety. Sections which may be of interest include:

Sect. 246 — Municipal Licenses.
Sect. 379, para. 86-88 — Trailer camps.
Sect. 352-395 — By-laws generally.

The Tourism Act, RSO 1970 Chapter 122

This affects all hotels in Ontario because under it they require a license to operate a tourist establishment by virtue of Section 6. It applies to premises providing sleeping accommodation. Other sections of interest include:

Sect. 1 (g) — Defines a tourist establishment which must provide sleeping accommodation.

Sect. 5 — Power of Minister to appoint an investigator to inquire into any matter connected with the tourist industry.

Sect. 6 — No new construction of tourist resorts or alteration of existing facilities except by permit issued under this Act.

Section 6a-6g — Licenses. A license is required to operate a tourist establishment.

Sect. 9 — Describes powers of inspectors under the Act.

Sect. 9a — Power of inspector to provisionally suspend a license.

Sect. 11 — Offenses and penalties.

Sect. 12 — Regulations.

The Elevators and Lifts Act, RSO 1970 Chapter 143

Sets standards for construction and use in regard to safety in the operation of elevators, lifts, hoists, dumb waiters, etc. As these are to be found in many hotels, this statute should be read.

The Industrial Safety Act, Ontario Statutes 1971 Chapter 43

This Act regulates safety in construction and occupancy of factories, shops and offices. Where a laundry is operated in conjunction with a hotel, it constitutes a factory by virtue of Section 1.

Sect. 8-14 — Deals with powers and duties of inspectors.

Sect. 22 — Duties of owner.

Sect. 28 — Employment of young persons.

Sect. 30 — Unsafe equipment.

Sect. 45 — Regulations.

Labour Relations Act, RSO 1970 Chapter 232

This statute was completely rewritten in 1970 and is the basic legislation relating to labour disputes. Hotel managers should be familiar with the general principles contained in the statute. The latest office consolidation can be obtained from the Department of Labour, Parliament Buildings, Toronto 2, Ontario.

The One Day's Rest in Seven Act, RSO 1970 Chapter 305

Regulates mandatory time off to be granted to employees. Particulars are contained in Section 2. Section 4 provides a penalty of $100.00 for contravention.

The Public Health Act, RSO 1970 Chapter 377

This act of 138 sections has the purpose of ensuring the safety of the public in respect to infectious diseases, unsanitary conditions and certain forms of pollution. Penalties run as high as $2,500.00 for some offenses.

The Workman's Compensation Act, RSO 1970 Chapter 505

Another important one for all employees. Hotel managers should again have some familiarity with it, as it will apply where employees may become entitled to compensation as a result of illness or injury in the course of their employment.

Index

Accidents
  automobile, 143, 145, 148
  investigation of, 32
  (See also Safety)
Administrative offices, security of,
  151-157
Alarm systems
  from contract service, 21, 23-24
  for emergency exits, 93
  fire, 176-177, 181-183, 185-186
  on fire doors, 177
  holdup, 23-24, 162, 164, 166
  for liquor storeroom, 99
  for maintenance areas, 199
  police response to, 37
  for records protection, 153
  theft prevention, 63-64, 131, 166
  for window protection, 60
Alcoholic beverage service, 95-112,
  128, 159, 198
  identifying stock, 101
  inspections in, 232
  laws governing, 46, 109-112, 213,
    App. A, 230-234
  licenses for, 109-111, App. A,
    231-232
  measuring liquor, 98, 102-104
  theft from, 96-97, 99-109
American Hotel/Motel Association,
  212, 215
Armored car service, 21, 23, 164
Arrest, of trespassers, 47
Arson, 53, 186-187
  (See also Fire and fire prevention)

Associations
  of hotel/motel operators, 40-41,
    212, 215
  of security personnel, 214-215
Automobiles
  damage to, 143, 145, 148
  searches of, 88-89, 118
  theft of, 143-144
  (See also Parking)

Banquets, 48, 137-138
Bellmen, 147-148
Bomb threats, 7, 191-193
  and evacuation, 7, 192-193
  law enforcement assistance in,
    191-192
  search procedures, 192
Bonding of employees, 22, 36, 103,
  155, 162

Cameras
  for check cashing, 171
  used during strikes, 200
  (See also Closed circuit television)
Cash
  protection of, 21, 23, 105-106,
    160-164
  theft of, 160
Cashiers, 160, 162-163
  in alcoholic beverage service,
    105-106
  dishonesty among, 171-172
  in food service department, 118
  in preventing fraud, 168, 170

239

About the authors. . . .

Walter J. Buzby II is a nationally known consultant to the hotel, motel, restaurant and bar industry as well as a fire and arson investigator. Chief Fire Investigator for the Atlantic County Board of Chosen Freeholders in New Jersey, he is a member of the County Prosecutor's Arson Task Force and Deputy Fire Coordinator.

Mr. Buzby has lectured and published extensively on hotel/motel security and fire prevention and investigation. He is an Adjunct Instructor in the Fire Science, Law Enforcement and Security Management Programs of Atlantic Community College. Professional memberships include the International Association of Arson Investigators, the Conference of Police Professionals, and the Cornell Society of Hotelmen.

David Paine is an Instructor in Law Enforcement and Industrial Security at Loyalist College of Applied Arts and Technology in Belleville, Ontario. During more than 30 years of security experience he has been Chief Security Officer for Air Transport Command with the Canadian Armed Forces; a member of the Metropolitan Police in London, England, for 8 years; and commander of a security unit in Egypt while in the British Army.

Mr. Paine has authored numerous articles on security and another book entitled *Basic Principles of Industrial Security.* He is also Canadian Correspondent for *Security Gazette,* a British publication. Professional affiliations include membership with the Canadian Society for Industrial Security.

Other Security World Books of Interest . . .

INTRODUCTION TO SECURITY, by Gion Green and Raymond C. Farber
Revised Edition
Comprehensive introduction to the history, nature and scope of security in modern society; basic principles and practices. 336 pages.

EFFECTIVE SECURITY MANAGEMENT, by Charles A. Sennewald
Comprehensive, practical guide to managing a security department in any company. 300 pages.

LOSS PREVENTION: CONTROLS AND CONCEPTS, by Saul D. Astor
Thought-provoking examination of loss prevention by a leading security professional. 273 pages.

COMPUTER SECURITY, by John M. Carroll
Total program of protection for EDP systems and facilities. 400 pages.

MANAGING EMPLOYEE HONESTY, by Charles R. Carson
Systematic approach to total accountability in any business. 230 pages.

AIRPORT, AIRCRAFT & AIRLINE SECURITY, by Kenneth C. Moore
Definitive study of every aspect of air traffic security. 356 pages.

BOMB SECURITY GUIDE, by Graham C. Knowles
Step-by-step emergency program against bombs and bomb threats. 157 pages.

CONFIDENTIAL INFORMATION SOURCES: PUBLIC & PRIVATE, by John M. Carroll
Unique guide to public and private personal records. 352 pages.

SUCCESSFUL RETAIL SECURITY, An Anthology
Over 25 top security and insurance professionals pool expertise. 303 pages.

OFFICE & OFFICE BUILDING SECURITY, by Ed San Luis
Security solutions for offices, high-rise buildings. 295 pages.

ALARM SYSTEMS & THEFT PREVENTION, by Thad L. Weber
Definitive treatment of alarm systems and problems. 385 pages.

INTERNAL THEFT: INVESTIGATION & CONTROL, An Anthology
Top security professionals analyze employee theft controls. 276 pages.

HOSPITAL SECURITY, by Russell L. Colling
Complete protection of people, property in health care facilities. 384 pages.

Books and other materials are available from Security World Publishing Co., Inc., 2639 S. La Cienega Blvd., Los Angeles, CA 90034.

45